"You're going to love this book! Pau... p... ways to combat the biggest lies twentysomethings are believing. He gives practical action steps through winsome and engaging stories. You won't be able to put it down. He inspires readers to ask the hard questions and see how integral their generation is to the world. If you pick up this book, get two and share it. It will be helpful to whoever reads it."

Jonathan Pokluda, author of *Outdated* and
bestseller *Welcome to Adulting*

"As someone who struggled with believing a lot of lies during my twenties, I cannot recommend this book highly enough. Paul Angone delivers so much truth in this book to combat the lies that can wreck our lives and relationships and keep us stifled from stepping out and using our gifts and talents to make a difference in this world."

Crystal Paine, *New York Times* bestselling author,
podcaster, and entrepreneur

"Life is confusing, especially in your twenties. This book will lead you out of the darkness and into the most thriving decade of your life. It's a must-read for any twentysomething, as well as teachers, friends, and parents of those who want to do more than wander."

Jeff Goins, bestselling author of *The Art of Work*

"'Miracles favor forward movement,' Paul Angone writes in *25 Lies*, and this book will help you ditch all the unhelpful baggage preventing momentum. Our twenties are a pivotal time for foundation setting, and yet for so many of us they are rife with insecurities and upheaval. Instead of finding the steady ground we so desperately seek, it's as if we're straddling the fault line of tectonic plates that are set on creating one identity-shaking quake after another. In another one of his masterpieces—or "happy little accidents"—Paul brings his signature wit, grit, heart, and grace to reveal twenty-five new secrets: that each of the biggest beliefs holding us back are just paper tigers waiting to be brought to light."

Jenny Blake, author of *Pivot: The Only Move That Matters Is Your Next One* and *Life after College*

"Just when you think you've got life figured out, the whole world gets turned upside down and you realize just how young and clueless you really are (just me?). Paul cuts through the crappy advice you see posted next to photos of white sand beaches on Instagram and nails the lies, fears, and insecurities I didn't even realize I was struggling with. Perfect read for anyone staring down their thirties like it's the deadline for becoming a 'real' adult. And if I had to pick one, my 'favorite lie' that always gets me is #4!"

Heath and Alyssa Padgett, hosts of *RV Entrepreneur* podcast and bestselling author of *Living in an RV*

"This is the book I wish I had in my twenties. It's hopeful. It's inspiring. Plus, it's packed with strategic insight into living a successful and meaningful life. If you're going through a full-blown quarter-life crisis or you just need a bit of a boost, this is a book all twentysomethings should read."

Jon Acuff, *New York Times* bestselling author of *Finish: Give Yourself the Gift of Done*

"What I love about this book is how Paul focuses on the mind and the stories we tell ourselves in our twenties. The stories we tell ourselves are often based on unsubstantiated claims, and Paul does a wonderful job of unpacking how we can go from 'what we feel like we are supposed to do in life' to 'who we are supposed to be in life.' It truly is a great guide for anyone who feels stuck in life."

Tayo Rockson, author of *Use Your Difference to Make a Difference*

25 LIES
TWENTYSOMETHINGS
NEED TO STOP BELIEVING

25 LIES TWENTYSOMETHINGS NEED TO STOP BELIEVING

HOW TO GET UNSTUCK AND OWN YOUR DEFINING DECADE

PAUL ANGONE

BakerBooks

a division of Baker Publishing Group
Grand Rapids, Michigan

© 2021 by Paul Angone

Published by Baker Books
a division of Baker Publishing Group
PO Box 6287, Grand Rapids, MI 49516-6287
www.bakerbooks.com

Printed in the United States of America

Library of Congress Cataloging-in-Publication Data
Names: Angone, Paul, author.
Title: 25 lies twentysomethings need to stop believing : how to get unstuck and own
    your defining decade / Paul Angone.
Other titles: Twenty-five lies twentysomethings need to stop believing
Description: Grand Rapids, Michigan : Baker Books, a division of Baker Publishing
    Group, [2021]
Identifiers: LCCN 2020035438 | ISBN 9781540900708 (paperback) | ISBN
    9781540901422 (casebound)
Subjects: LCSH: Young adults—Life skills guides. | Common fallacies.
Classification: LCC HQ799.5 .A54 2021 | DDC 646.70084/2—dc23
LC record available at https://lccn.loc.gov/2020035438

The author is represented by The Christopher Ferebee Agency, www. christopherferebee.com.

21 22 23 24 25 26 27   7 6 5 4 3 2 1

In keeping with biblical principles of creation stewardship, Baker Publishing Group advocates the responsible use of our natural resources. As a member of the Green Press Initiative, our company uses recycled paper when possible. The text paper of this book is composed in part of post-consumer waste.

To my daughter, Jlynn Joy.
May your life be filled with truth,
wisdom, and overflowing joy.

Contents

INTRODUCTION
Out on a Ledge

"Where is that shouting coming from?" I turn to my wife as I pause our late-night Netflix binge.

"It sounds like it's right outside our balcony." My wife glances toward our toddlers' bedroom, hoping the noise doesn't wake them up.

We live in a sleepy San Diego condo community made up of young families and retirees. Screams and shouts at 10:30 p.m. are not the norm. We step outside on our second-story back balcony to see what the commotion is. And in an instant, we enter into a life-or-death standoff like I've never experienced before.

Diagonally above us in the third-story condo and to our left, our neighbor is standing on his balcony railing that is as narrow as a balance beam. Two police officers below. A police officer at the opening of the door to the balcony. If he falls, he's at a distance that will either kill him or break every bone in his body.

Our neighbor is frantically yelling that he is going to jump.

From the shouts going back and forth, the police are there because of something our neighbor has done.

Our neighbor says he's done nothing wrong.

The shouts and screams escalate as our neighbor yells that he's not carrying a weapon, so the police officer should lower his gun.

11

Then our neighbor, quite amazingly, while balancing on the railing, takes off all his clothes down to his underwear to show he's not carrying a weapon. He throws everything to the street below. He's almost naked. Is it so he can leave this world the same way he came in? It's what I start fearing. There I am. About twenty feet away. I can see my neighbor and he can see me. We've said hi a few times in the past as he walks his dog, but I don't know his name. I kick myself for not knowing it. The cops have blocked off the whole area. Other than the police, I'm the only other person he can talk to. For some reason, the police let me stay there.

As the madness and desperation come in bigger, successive waves, there are moments my heart leaps into my throat as his feet hang off the edge. Moments he stares down and gets very quiet. Those are the moments that feel like eternity.

The back-and-forth negotiations are not going well. I wonder if I should just tuck away inside. I'm guessing the official stance is that I shouldn't be interfering in police business. I wonder if I'm going to make things worse. What if he talks to me and I say something wrong?

What do I do? Go back inside to our Netflix show and turn up the volume? How can I *not* be there? To at least be someone he can talk to who is not a police officer. I am here for a reason. Or at least that's what I keep telling myself as the other part of me is telling me to go back inside and close the blinds.

As I watch my neighbor's emotions go from rage to mourning, I feel like I'm watching all his hopes, failures, and fears play out right in front of me.

I pray my two little girls don't wake up to witness this. I pray for my neighbor standing on that railing. I pray for something to say. For hours I stay there, trying to formulate some answer, some magical phrase in my head in case he brings me into the conversation. But nothing is coming to mind.

How many lies has this man believed about his life, his purpose, his relationships, his childhood that have led him to this moment where one step forward won't be progress, but death? How do I speak into his life? What are the right words to say?

Then it happens.

I'll finish the rest of this story a little further below.

Lies, the Ledge, and a Loss of Sight

Why start a book about the "lies we believe in our twenties" with this intense story of my neighbor on a ledge?

We all meet people who are on the ledge in some way, in less drastic or obvious conditions. We all come across people who feel purposeless and feel alone.

Sometimes that person is us.

I know I've been on a figurative ledge at some points in my life, not wanting to jump, yet not knowing how to go back inside. I've been gripped by the hopelessness that feels like you're running out of options. That there is no escape. That this is it. This is your life.

In my midtwenties, I was on a trajectory toward rock bottom. Everything I thought I knew, I didn't know anymore. At least rock bottom would be sturdy. At least there would be no place to go but up, right?

Yet, as I fell toward the bottom, instead I smacked down on a ledge. A ledge of grace. It didn't feel like grace at the time. It felt like hard ground where I lay broken. Lying there on the ledge, I knew a bunch of lies had brought me there. The fruit of those lies was like that three-week-old banana you stumble across in the back of your car—black and mushy, emitting a terrible smell.

On the ledge, I had a decision. Did I roll right and continue my free fall, holding onto these lies like plastic-bag-parachutes with big rips in them? Or did I ditch all those bags? Did I free my hands? Did I begin the long, slow climb back to truth—whatever or wherever that might be?

I chose to climb back toward truth. I'm still on that climb. That's been the journey of my last decade where I've studied, researched, and written the books *101 Secrets for Your Twenties, All Groan Up,* and *101 Questions You Need to Ask in Your Twenties.*

I still believe our twenties and thirties are the most crucial decades of our life. So why a book about lies we believe in our twenties and even our thirties? Well, if we don't start there, how do we get to truth, how do we set the foundation in these defining decades of our lives?

Lies are dangerous. Mainly when we don't see them as such.

The Danger of Lies

The most dangerous kinds of lies are the ones we live as truths.

A lie, defined as a lie, is harmless. Like a lion in a cage at the zoo. We know what damage it can do. But it's behind glass. Even though it is staring at us like it wishes we were its midday snack, it cannot hurt us (or at least, we hope that glass surrounding it is as strong as they say).

No, it is the lies that are living with us but we don't see as lies—those are the ones that can maim us spiritually, emotionally, mentally, and physically. It is the lion we invite into our homes, thinking its time at the zoo has rid it of its human-eating desires. Then we find out with some shock that it would rather devour us than the porkchop we gave it for lunch on our new Target Hearth & Hand plates.

> We are living under a tyranny of untruth. The basic falsehood is the lie that we are totally dedicated to truth.
>
> —Thomas Merton

The lies we live with are the lies that will destroy where we live. These lies will take our home and heart, and turn them into places of unrest. Too many of us have invited too many lies into our homes. Too many lions prowling in our halls and we wonder why we can't sleep.

When the Many Become One

These lies aren't as obvious as inviting lions into our house. Maybe instead it's simply a bad habit we've convinced ourselves is not a big deal. Yet, over days and months it keeps dripping in our house, like a leaky faucet we don't have the time or energy to fix. This lie drips and drips. Before we realize the damage it's doing, it warps everything around it and turns it into black mold.

Or maybe the lie starts becoming a part of us, like a skin graft where we can no longer separate our own skin from the imposter. These are the lies I'm concerned about. These are the lies we must call out by name and remove. We cannot let them take up a dangerous, raging residence in our minds and hearts.

These lies are waiting to take our identity, strength, empathy, hope, and purpose to a cheese grater and turn them into unrecognizable bits and pieces. If it feels like I'm using heightened metaphors and images when describing the negative effects these lies can have on our lives, well, it's because I am. Lies and truth are death and life. Especially in our twenties.

In your twenties you are deciding everything. The canvas is blank.

To Truth or to Untruth?

You are building the foundation of your life in your twenties and thirties. If your foundation is riddled with cracks or on uneven land, what will happen later to the house you're building?

How can we build on lies and expect our future to be well built? The whole thing, no matter how impressive it looks at times, will come crashing down.

Your twenties are the most important time to ask hard questions and identify and remove the lies that are messing up your foundation. Too many people I meet in their fifties and sixties have spent the last forty years of their lives trying to fix the unintentional, ill-thought, ignorant, and arrogant decisions they made in their twenties. They built their entire lives on a flimsy foundation of lies and are still paying for it.

Dare to Be Wise

In this book I'm going to define and discuss some of the most prevalent, yet subtle lies that I've seen hold people back based on all my conversations, research, and experience over the last two decades working with twentysomethings and thirtysomethings. Then after defining the lie, we will get down to the truth.

We're all struggling in some way. We act like we have it all figured out on the outside, then alone in our room at night we feel like we're still that scared ten-year-old, listening to our parents fighting outside our door, wishing someone would come to help.

Let's help each other expose the lies and uncover the truth. There's too much riding on this decade. We're looking at the rest of our lives. We need some truth to help light that dark, windy path we're all staring at. We can't go at this alone. We need people walking next to us to pick us up when we face-plant. We need truth-tellers walking next to us.

You can't do this alone. You're not supposed to.

Beware of false knowledge; it is more dangerous than ignorance.
—George Bernard Shaw

16

Back on the Ledge

For hours I stand on my balcony, experiencing my neighbor battling with these lies. The emotions he displays as he stands on that ledge are extreme in every way.

From rage—pounding a wall as he cusses out anyone in sight or in memory.

To madness—taking down huge wind chimes and furiously shaking them so loudly that they ring across the condo complex like a sadistic church bell. Grabbing his head and screaming for the officer to just shut up.

To fear and desperation—frantically searching for any escape. For any way out of this.

To deep sorrow, regret, and full realization—crouching on the railing, sobbing and saying over and over again, "I'm done. I'm done."

My neck, shoulders, and legs throb, as they've been in a permanent state of tension for hours. I can only imagine how his legs must be feeling, standing on that narrow ledge. And even if he doesn't jump, at some point is he going to lose his balance and fall?

After hours of being present, searching my mind for something to say in case my neighbor tries to connect with me, he finally calls down to me. My heart leaps into my throat as I still don't know what to say or do.

Without thinking, something comes from my soul more than from my brain, and I looked up at him and said, "I care about you. And I don't want to see you get hurt. I'm here for you and I care about you."

That was it.

As my words reached him, his body relaxed. His voice quieted down. I watched the intensity leave as he took a deep breath and looked up at the sky.

I don't think I magically saved the day. But something about hearing those words "I'm here for you and I care about you" had a

> If conscience disapproves, the loudest applauses of the world are of little value.
>
> —John Adams

noticeable effect on him. After four hours, he simply stepped down. Not to the cement below, but to the police officers in his condo. The standoff was over. Unceremoniously and in an instant. He found enough truth to step down to life.

Step into Hope, Joy, and Truth

To some extent, it feels like the whole world is standing on the ledge. Not wanting to jump, but not knowing how to step back down.

Yet, there's power in telling someone that you care about them and are there for them. No matter what. I hope that is what this book and conversation is for all of us. A place of rest. A place to talk and listen. A place to clean out the lies so we can live a good life.

As we stand on this ledge together, I reach out my hand. Let's step together into hope, real joy, truth, and life. Let's step into freedom as we cut off the lies that have locked us down too long.

Let's put the lions in their proper place. Truth is a stubborn thing. Let's search for it and invite it in for dinner. Who knows, we might be surprised by what it has to say.

LIE #1
Success just happens

Remember Bob Ross? He's the soothing painter of "happy little trees" that created a whopping thirty-one seasons of *The Joy of Painting*. The show ran nationwide on PBS stations, making it arguably the most popular art instruction show of all time.

Even if Bob Ross was before your time, you've probably come across him in meme form as his famous Afro and sayings have lived on far beyond him. If you have no idea who I'm talking about, go find an episode of *The Joy of Painting* and enjoy.

Bob's mission was to make art accessible to everyone. He used his TV show to teach people the techniques as he created a peaceful landscape right in front of you. His secret to painting was layering colors on top of each other on the canvas.

But his show was much more than that. I watched a great documentary about his life called *The Happy Painter*, where I learned that out of the millions who watched his show, only about 10 to 15 percent actually were painting along with him. Most people just watched him without ever picking up a brush. Even now, reruns of his show are everywhere, and you have twenty-somethings born after his death still appreciating Bob Ross and his joy of painting.

But why? Why was his show so popular, even to non-painters? I can only imagine pitching his show concept now to TV execs.

"Okay, so picture this. We're going to get this tall white guy with an Afro who sounds like he's ushering in songs on the nine-to-eleven p.m. shift on the soft jazz station. We're going to put him on a stool in front of a black drop cloth. Then get this, he's going to paint a painting for an hour and talk about it! It's going to be huge!"

So in an age of instant, fast-paced, high drama and intrigue, how is Bob Ross still resonating? Well, if I was going to theorize, I'd say these things:

1. Because everything feels so crazy in our lives and in the world, to listen and watch Bob Ross create this peaceful world in front of you feels like you're visiting the best psychologist money can't buy.

2. He's so upbeat and encouraging, he's like this calm mentor reassuring you that everything is going to be okay. Just keep painting.

3. Watching him go from blank canvas to beautiful painting in an hour feels magical. In a world of constant incompleteness, watching Bob Ross finish something beautiful feels incredibly satisfying.

4. He makes you feel like you can also paint happy little trees.

Why in a book for today's twentysomethings am I talking at length about Bob Ross? Well, for many reasons.

Success in your twenties is a lot like a Bob Ross painting.

You start with a blank canvas. It feels like everyone is watching. You create by putting one layer on top of another. And along the way, there will be many happy little accidents or crappy little failures, depending on what you do with them.

When the blemishes come, it's your choice to scrap the whole thing and start over. Or turn the happy little accidents into a beautiful tree or a "purposefully" placed bush.

The Power of Happy Little Accidents

Actually, Bob's whole show and brand was one happy little accident after another.

Bob didn't set out to be a TV star who would later appear on the *Phil Donahue Show* and *Live! with Regis and Kathie Lee*, among many others. No, Bob just wanted to be an art instructor. And he was traveling around the nation for years, trying (rather unsuccessfully) to sell seats to his live art workshops. Money was so tight that Bob got an idea for how he could save a few hundred bucks a year: perm his straight hair and just let it grow out. That way he wouldn't have to get haircuts!

Then one day, while trying to sell seats to a workshop in Indiana, he got the idea to see if the local public TV station would film an infomercial for him to promote his workshop. He filmed it and filled seats to his workshop, and a producer loved him so much, they asked him if he would like to turn it into a show. Thus, *The Joy of Painting*.

But when the show started taking off, there was one thing that really bugged Bob Ross—his hair! He was completely embarrassed by it, but the producers wouldn't let him cut it because it would mess up the continuity of the season.

Soon the hair he wanted to change, he realized, was the exact thing that people remembered most about him. And he'd fully embraced the look, making his Afro his trademark logo on all his painting products.

Bob Ross is a lesson that **your peculiarities are priceless.** What we see as embarrassments, others see as our unique gift. What we want to hide is actually what others are most drawn to.

Bob's TV show and his hair were two happy little accidents that Bob Ross built his success on.

Magic Is the Least Magical Thing There Is

Also, and I say this as a compliment, while it felt like Bob Ross was creating magic in that hour on the canvas, it was actually not

21

magic at all. Yes, Bob Ross painted that entire painting in an hour. This is true. But he wasn't just starting the painting from scratch. When he got in front of that camera and began his painting that he'd complete on camera, he'd already painted the exact painting that was sitting in front of him off camera. He'd worked out where everything should go. He fixed the perspective and the sight lines. He masterfully and skillfully constructed the painting in his workshop, then he brought in the finished painting that stood in front of him off camera that he would reference throughout the show.

He wasn't being magical. He was being a master at his craft. And this is not even mentioning that before he ever got in front of a camera, he had trained and studied for years under a master painter. He taught hundreds of people through small live workshops to learn all the techniques and tricks to make something as joyful and magical as creating a beautiful painting.

While Bob Ross was creating magic on screen, he'd worked diligently and skillfully to create a space and skill set to allow that magic to happen.

Magic never just happens.

Actually, magic is the least magical thing there is.

What we see as magic is someone's years and years of painstakingly perfecting their craft.

The master magician is the least magical person in the room. The magician is probably just the hardest-working person in the room and has excelled the best at learning through failure to perfect a craft that looks flawless.

It takes many years of hard work to make something hard look easy.

> **Once you have the technique down, all you need is the dream in your heart and the desire to put it on canvas.**
> —Bob Ross

The same principle applies for other magical people we marvel at. The speaker who is able to get on stage and mesmerize a crowd. The business leader who is able to make a wise, strategic decision in the face of uncertainty. The comedian who is able to get an auditorium rolling in laughter every twenty seconds for an hour. The parent who is able to truly hear what their child is saying and speak to their heart in return. The basketball player who makes ten three-point baskets in a row. The chef who creates a dish that people are making reservations six months out to experience. The writer who wraps you up in a story that you can't put down. All of this is magic. Yet, it's not magical at all. None of it just happens. What we see as magic is the by-product of years of mastery.

Becoming Better

I heard Jerry Seinfeld say on the *What a Joke with Papa and Fortune* show that he was about to film his next hour special in 2020. He'd filmed his last hour special in 2001. Seinfeld joked half seriously, "Give me twenty good years of hard work and I'll give you a killer hour." While he admitted that his timeline might be a little extreme, he did argue that he felt like it takes most good comedians five years of really perfecting their routine before they are ready for their "hour special." And he felt most specials today are rushed too quickly and are most likely money grabs, and the lack of quality is apparent.

Jerry Seinfeld doesn't get up on *The Tonight Show* and have the audience riveted by just naturally being funny. No, he perfected every sentence, every pause of those five minutes, at hundreds of clubs in New York. Then shows in Fort Lauderdale. At a show that semi bombed in Austin, Texas. In LA, Denver, Portland, etc., etc. He hammered out that routine like a master blacksmith making a decorative trellis. Then one night he says an off-beat comment at a show in Mesa, Arizona, that gets everyone howling and he's just stumbled across a happy little accident through persistence, practice, and vulnerability.

If you never allow yourself to operate in a space where failure and embarrassment are a very real possibility, then you'll never be in a place where success is a real possibility either.

Miracles Favor Forward Movement

"Magic" happens through years of perseverance, intentionality, humility, and gritty, hard work when no one is watching. That's where the real magic happens.

Miracles find a way of showing up for those who have been working hard enough at their craft that they know when a miracle has just come across their path.

Miracles show up for someone who has completely emptied themselves to allow space for something extraordinary to take place.

People usually catch their big breaks after they've been broken.

Bob Ross created magic through years of hard work mastering his craft and many "happy little accidents" along the way that he embraced instead of erased.

Sure, sometimes people stumble across some successful outcome. Success happens to a lot of people, but they have no capacity, strength, or foundation to build from it. Because it was a piece of fleeting magic to them and they have no idea how to sustain it.

NEXT STEPS:

- Be like Bob Ross. Are you going to let the mis-strokes of life be crappy little failures or happy little accidents? The choice is up to you, no one else. Are you going to let the struggle become part of your story or are you going to silence your struggle because you're embarrassed by it? Embrace all the happy little accidents. Don't erase them, embrace them.

- Success doesn't just happen. It's a meticulous, consistent process. Success is like making wine. You need to squeeze a lot of grapes and tinker with a lot of recipes before you get anything worth drinking and sharing with others.

- What we see as embarrassing, others see as our signature touch: that crack in your voice; that nose that seems to protrude too far; that learning disability you've had to struggle through; your rough upbringing; how you seem to create, think, speak, write, dance unlike anyone else, no matter how hard you've tried to conform. If anything is magic, this is it. *Your peculiarities are priceless.*

- What we see as setbacks are what make us unique and inspiring to others. Case in point, Bob's Afro. As simple as it sounds to even state this, what sets you apart is what sets you apart. Too many of us are trying to discard what makes us priceless.

- And if you need a soothing voice to encourage you along the way, call a friend. Or if your friends aren't picking up, find an episode of *The Joy of Painting* and you might discover a nugget of truth from Bob Ross as he paints a tree, then paints another right next to it, because "even trees need a friend."

LIE #2

I'm an incapable human being who is incapable of doing things that most capable people can do // a.k.a. I suck

Have you experienced this weird phenomenon? When you're about to embark on important work, then all of a sudden you're questioning every single life choice that's brought you to that moment. Every insecurity that you thought you were over starts buzzing in your ear like a hoard of belligerent wasps.

About five minutes into working, you find yourself giving up: "Okay, okay, I'll start scrolling through another social media feed! And I'll put something on from Netflix. Just stop yelling at me!"

You see, the Liar doesn't want you to do important work. That's when its voice gets the strongest. Why? Because the Liar doesn't want you to risk. The Liar is that "friend" who's always telling you "That won't work," trying to project their own fear on you like you're a drive-in movie theater screen.

Well, if we're going to tackle lies, if we're going to set ourselves up to succeed, build, and create, we first have to tackle the Liar. Because the Liar's one goal is to make you believe that you don't have what it takes.

Steven Pressfield, in his seminal book *The War of Art*, describes the battle creatives face as fighting against Resistance. The truth is, whether you call yourself a creative or not, we all get body slammed at times by the Liar. I know I do. Here are some things the Liar shouts at me:

Who are you to write another book?

Who are you to inspire and encourage people?

I think you've written all you can. You might want to start looking at another career.

The Liar wants to take you out at that starting line. The Truth-Teller wants you to take that first step into the race. It can't guarantee you're going to win, but it can guarantee that if you give up at the starting line, you're for sure, 100 percent going to come in last place.

The Liar wants to dump all your insecurities and fears on you, especially when you're trying to fall asleep. The Truth-Teller just wants you to go to bed at a reasonable time and actually get some rest.

The Liar wants you to try and find happiness by seeking happiness for happiness' sake. The Truth-Teller wants you to find joy by doing meaningful work and helping others.

The Liar wants you to conform and blend in like a chameleon. The Truth-Teller wants to raise your colors like a peacock and give the world a new masterpiece.

The Liar wants you to waste time. The Truth-Teller wants you to invest your time wisely.

The Liar wants you to stay in a cage where it's safe. The Truth-Teller wants you to soar.

The Liar wants you to believe it's too late. The Truth-Teller laughs and says you've got like sixty years ahead. *What the heck is the Liar talking about?!*

The Liar wants you to see other people's snapshots of success and be jealous. The Truth-Teller wants to applaud your friend's success and let it inspire you to keep taking chances.

The Liar wants you to treat hope as a feeling. The Truth-Teller wants you to treat hope as a fact.

The Liar wants you to pay attention only to the voices of other liars. The Truth-Teller wants you to listen to the wise.

The Liar wants you to believe that you can't escape *this*. The Truth-Teller gives a loving laugh and puts its hand on your shoulder to say, "You're not locked up in a maximum security prison here. Look, the door is wide open. All you have to do is walk out."

Even when you succeed, the Liar wants you to start worrying that you'll never be able to repeat it, that the success was a fluke. The Truth-Teller doesn't want you to repeat it. The Truth-Teller wants you to calmly build off of it, with freedom to let it become something completely new.

The Liar wants to paint you as a failure. The Truth-Teller wants to give you the grace to fail without calling yourself a failure.

The Liar doesn't want you to succeed. The Liar likes things just the way they are. The Liar doesn't like change because it is scared and insecure. It doesn't want you listening to the truth, because then it would lose all control. The Liar wants you to stay safely miserable, like a boat that's forever tied up in the harbor and never ventures out to sea.

But here's the thing—the storm can still get you in the harbor. And since you're tied up, you have no way of maneuvering away from the damaging winds. You just sit there and take it while the Liar lays back in its lawn chair, smoking its cigar and checking you off its list.

The Liar's voice is powerful, yet I believe the Truth-Teller's voice is even more so, if we only let ourselves listen to it.

That's why when I'm being attacked by the Liar, I repeat a line from the wise, truth-telling Mother Teresa:

> If you're truly humble, nothing will touch you, neither praise nor disgrace, because you know what you are.

Letting the Liar call the shots is like letting a wrecking ball paint your house. It doesn't make much sense. Sure, paint might get splattered around here and there, but it's going to be on a bunch of shattered pieces.

Here's the thing I've come to understand: I don't have what it takes. Yet, I do have what it takes. In some ways I will fail. In other ways I won't. Some pages I'll write and my wife will read them and try to find a polite way to say that the world is better off never seeing them. Then other pages she'll read and she'll be brought to tears. That's the process of writing a book. That's the process of becoming a better writer.

We battle the Liar with a humble confidence. We hold our life's dreams with an open hand and say, "Yeah, I don't know if this is going to work. But I'm going to try anyway."

Because most likely it's not going to work out like we thought, and instead, it's going to work out bigger and better than we ever could've imagined or hoped.

You speak to the Liar with truth. Over and over. Until the Liar's voice grows faint and the Truth-Teller's voice becomes yours.

NEXT STEPS:

- Know whenever you start on the path of doing something important, the Liar will try and take you out.
- Whose voice do you think you're listening more to in a day—the Liar's or the Truth-Teller's? Work on listening more to the Truth-Teller's voice in your mind rather than the Liar's. Just like any habit, it takes practice and time to change your previous default.
- To help you build that habit, find more truth-tellers in your life as well. We all need wise counselors, mentors, authors, and advisors in our lives. Sometimes the only way to spot

the Liar's voice is through a truth-teller pointing it out to you.

- It's hard to create anything worth creating if you listen to the Liar's voice while you create.
- Write down the thought-script running through your mind throughout the day. What are lies and what are truths?
- If we let fear and insecurities call the shots, what kind of life are we going to live?

LIE #3

I'm the only one struggling

Life in your twenties is like experiencing puberty all over again.

It's awkward.

It's confusing.

All your friends *appear* to be handling it better than you.

Feeling abnormal is the new normal.

Your body is going through changes as you learn the Freshman Fifteen is nothing compared to the Cubicle Cincuenta.

And you'd gladly just call in sick again and watch eight hours of a '90s sitcom. For three days straight.

Can you relate?

Like we did during puberty when that zit went all Mount St. Helens on the tip of our nose, we hide away. Yet in today's world, we're hiding in plain sight on social media.

The Paradox of See-Me Social Media

I was discussing this with my wife, and I felt like she encapsulated the paradox of social media perfectly in one quick line:

Social media is "I want to hide but still be seen."

A bunch of us hiding in plain sight, fully visible, yet hidden. Seen, but not known. Struggling, yet acting like we have all our stuff together.

We used to talk about having a FOMO—Fear of Missing Out—as a driving fear impacting decisions and the inability to commit to anything.

Yet, now I think we have taken it to a different level where we are having FOLS—a Fear of Looking Small or maybe a Fear of Looking Stupid. We carry around this secret fear of "if they only really knew how insignificant I was feeling." "If they only really knew the doubts and depression I'm going through." "If they only knew how insecure I really feel." "If they only knew my addictions." "If they only knew the truth . . . they wouldn't like me or care."

A stark lie that is hard to dispose of. Like getting pine sap on your hands, it's hard to wash this lie off.

And this goes for someone with 100 followers to 100 million. We all can carry around that secret shame of what people would think if they really saw the *me* behind the *social media me*.

Really, it's not too different from the timeless story of a rock star or famous actress/actor who is spiraling out of control. "If they only saw me when I stepped offstage or behind the screen."

We crave being seen. To justify our existence. To validate our worth. Especially during those seasons when we feel most unsure or insecure.

Yet, the amount of people who "see" you is never enough. No amount of likes will ever fill that void. It will never be enough. And the sheer amount of people seeing you usually has a direct correlation with the *lack* of people who truly know you.

You hear this time and time again from celebrities who are seen more than anyone, yet lament how few people they can trust and who really know them. It's hard for them to have meaningful relationships because they never know if someone likes them *for them* or likes them for the attention, fame, and money they bring. That's why celebrities typically stick the closest with the friends and family of their past, before the fame—people who really know where they came from and who they are. They are seen by millions, and that level of visibility that they fought for now becomes a heavy burden they can't escape.

The Age of Social Solitary Confinement

Solitary confinement is used as a torture technique. It is a tactic of breaking someone down by taking away all their human interactions. And studies have shown that it doesn't take long for solitary confinement to make an otherwise sane person start imagining a legion of squirrels wearing suits coming at them to steal their nuts.

As author and researcher Michael Bond writes, "What is known is that social isolation unleashes an extreme immune response—a cascade of stress hormones and inflammation."[1]

Keron Fletcher, a consultant psychiatrist who has helped debrief and treat hostages who were rescued from solitary confinement, says this about the by-products of the experience: "Hopelessness and helplessness are horrible things to live with and they erode morale and coping ability."[2]

So why do so many of us walk ourselves into that cell and toss out the key? Solitary confinement is used for enemies of the state. But we become our own biggest enemies when we purposefully confine and hide ourselves behind a screen. We isolate ourselves, then lament the fact that we feel so isolated.

We build our own prison walls, usually constructing them with happy social media posts about how epic (and enviable) our lives are. Then we lie down with our phones, feeling more afraid and alone than ever. The front door is wide open. We can easily escape. We see people laughing and enjoying life through our windows, yet we stay inside and hide.

Hiding from our relationships when they don't even know we're expecting them to find us.

Hiding from our dreams, because who are we to have them?

Hiding from that person we like, because frogs can't talk to swans.

Hiding from that awkward, uncomfortable feeling of trying something new—of openly becoming the novice who is hungry to learn—instead of hiding as the "expert" who knows it all.

Hiding from the truth we know in our hearts, because we can't stop listening to all the lies in our head.

Hiding from our authentic self, because we keep staring at the skewed image of ourselves like we're staring at a carnival mirror.

Hiding from our friends, because they are experiencing all the success we were "supposed to."

We hide while desperately wanting to be seen. We struggle, yet act like we're not struggling. It's really hard to live like that.

Sitting in the Circle

For the last two years, one of the most important things I've done is to meet with a group of guys every Wednesday at 7:00 a.m. We're not reading a book together. No one is really leading or teaching us. So why do I get up early every week to make it there?

Well, there's free coffee. That's a perk for sure. Then we sit in a circle and we each take a turn talking about what's going on in our lives. What we're struggling with. Thinking about. Excited about. Whatever. We simply "check in" with each other. Sometimes guys offer a piece of advice or an encouraging word. But mainly, we just sit and listen. It's such a simple hour, yet I've found it's a really important one for my whole week.

Why?

Well, if we're really honest with ourselves, it's because we all have this deep desire to know and be known.

To sit in a circle, look each other in the face, and take a collective breath together. It's awkward and vulnerable at first. Old pubescent insecurities pop up, screaming at you to casually go to the bathroom and just never come back to the group again. Yet, it's a profound reminder for all of us that we're not alone.

To know and be known is like a tether cord that ties an astronaut to his ship. With all the fancy tools and technologies we have today, sitting in this circle where I can be honest with others becomes that cord that keeps me from floating away.

I believe our future, our well-being, and our impact will hinge on whether we allow ourselves to take rest in this simple human truth . . . to know and be known. To connect with each other over our shared struggle.

Whether we are thirteen or thirty-one or ninety-one, this need, this truth never changes. We need it like water. Yet so many of us are trying to survive on just a few drops a month. We're all struggling. Yet again, too many of us are struggling to make it appear like we're not struggling.

I think we all perceive our blemishes to be much bigger, more glaring, and more disgusting than others do. We stare at our imperfections like we're Rudolph the Red-Nosed Reindeer, when others just see the light we emit that they wish they could too. But they do—they just can't see it either!

Our skewed view of self is skewering us. Are we using social media as a way to be seen? Or are we using it as a flashy way to hide?

We are not alone in this. Are we allowing others to really see us beyond what is seen? To really know us. The beautiful and the flawed.

Right now, I invite us all to go to that circle together. To experience life with each other in our own perfect imperfection. Transitions are awkward for all of us. When everything you used to depend on feels like it's falling apart, you're going to need someone to lean on. We all do.

To know and be known. It's a core part of our humanness. It puts its arm around our loneliness and says, "You're not alone."

NEXT STEPS:

- We hide while desperately wanting to be seen. It's really hard to live like that. Are there ways you feel like you're hiding even though you're extremely visible on social media? Social media can be a great tool to authentically connect with others if we're able to be authentic on it. We'll talk more about that later on in the book.

- We all need to know and be known. Are you putting yourself in places where you can get to know people and they can get to know you? Maybe it's time to let yourself feel a little awkward and seek out new opportunities for community through a hobby or activity you enjoy, a meet-up group, religious organization, local volunteering opportunities, political involvement, or just a more intentional effort on your part to get to know your neighbors around you.

LIE #4
I've missed my chance

I was searching the bargain basement bin in an old shop building close to where I live, when something caught my eye—a book from 1883 of letters and poems from the famous Scottish poet Robert Burns. He is best known in the Western world for writing "Auld Lang Syne," which we sing on New Year's Eve as we hopefully look forward to the new year.

Yet, Robert Burns wasn't exactly the friend you'd be inviting over to really get your New Year's Eve party started. As I read through Burns's personal letters, one letter particularly that Burns wrote to his father struck me: "I foresee that poverty and obscurity probably await me and I am in some measure prepared and daily preparing to meet them."[1]

The certainty of this line really struck me. I thought, *When did Robert Burns write this letter to his father?* It must have been near his deathbed, as he feared his work would enter into obscurity. So I looked up when Robert Burns was born and compared it to the date on the letter. I was shocked! Burns wrote to his father that poverty and obscurity awaited him when he was twelve years old. Twelve!

First, I hope my kids' vocabulary is rocking enough at twelve that they know words like poverty and obscurity. Second, I really hope my kids aren't writing me a letter like this, sure of their destitution at twelve years old when the rest of their lives await them! The next time you sing "Auld Lang Syne," make a toast to Robert Burns. He was right about many things, but his hopelessness about the lack of impact he was going to make was a lie.

Taking Pictures in a Meat Locker

I think of another young man who was losing hope at a frightening rate. He was in his early twenties and life was just not turning out the way he felt it was "supposed to." His band had finally made their first heavy metal music album and it was a flop. The album cover of these two long-haired outcasts standing in a meat locker with big chunks of dead cow hanging around felt like a pretty accurate picture of this musician's career and future.

Plus, not only was his music career failing, his love life was falling apart as well. Why is it that when one goes, the other closely follows? So with his present looking bleak and the real possibility that he would not make it as a heavy metal artist, the man decided to succumb to the ultimate lie and take his own life. At twenty-one years old, like Robert Burns at twelve, he was sure his life was over even though he'd lived so little of it. He'd lost all hope.

Thankfully, his attempt at suicide was not successful, and he would begin the slow, steady climb out. Maybe there was hope for him after all. Maybe heavy metal just wasn't the best medium for him to explore his music. He was trying to sing like the lead singer from Led Zeppelin, and maybe the real problem was that he needed to find his own sound.

So he began exploring more songs featuring his piano playing. He began writing authentic lyrics about the struggle he was going through. And as he literally escaped from New York to LA, attempting to go into exile to rid himself of another failed relationship with his manager, he played piano. A complete unknown in a smoky Los Angeles bar. And that's where he wrote his first hit.[2]

Since then, he's sold more than 150 million albums, has received 23 Grammy nominations, and has sold more albums than Bruce Springsteen, Michael Jackson, and Madonna.[3]

This heavy-metal-playing musician who had lost hope, then turned to his piano to help tell his story? Billy Joel. And his first real hit that he wrote while living in near exile, playing to hungover people in an LA bar? "Piano Man."

We lose hope much too quickly. We become sure of our defeat when we haven't even started the race.

You have so much waiting for you. Even if you can't see it right now, it's there, waiting with a knowing smirk. I promise. You can believe in hope. You can cling to it when the ship feels like it's going down. We must. If we don't hope in our future, then our future will feel shipwrecked before it's even had the chance to leave the harbor.

The Redemption of *Shawshank Redemption*

I think of the final powerful scene of the movie *Shawshank Redemption*. Throughout the movie, best friends Andy Dufresne and Red fight about only one thing. Something that makes Red slam his plate down in disgust and walk away from Andy. That one thing that drives a wedge between them? Hope.

Red argues that hope is "a dangerous thing. Hope can drive a man insane." While Andy argues that hope "is a good thing, maybe the best of things, and no good thing ever dies."[4]

While Andy sat surrounded by the hard, cold reality of prison, he had a vision of his future, fixing up an old boat on the Mexican beaches of Zihuatanejo and taking tourists out on fishing trips. More than just a dream, Andy spoke of this vision with such detail, it was like it was already happening.

Lost in My Own Prison

At twenty-five years old, I had already been rejected by more publishers than many people are turned down by in their lifetime. Every day I waited for that email of the "yes!" that would change my life while I worked various wild jobs to make ends meet. That email of yes never came.

So I completely started over. I ended my contract with my literary agent at the time. I started a master's program. Then I was hired at the same university, which would also help pay for my master's, for an experimental position where I would work at two different campuses under two different bosses in two different positions, forty-five minutes away from each other.

I was a guinea pig for this new hybrid/"we are mainly trying to save money" position. And I quickly learned that guinea pigs don't have a long lifespan. I was skewered and roasted like a Peruvian delicacy.

To make a long story short, I would be called into Human Resources (in only two weeks!) to find both my bosses sitting there with the director of HR. There, one boss called me "insubordinate and incompetent" and wanted me fired. The other boss said I was doing a great job and was ready to welcome me with open arms.

So I shifted full-time to the main campus but would still need to have a working relationship with my previous boss who just fired me. Fun, awkward times.

Finding a Life-Saving Truth-Teller

During all this time, I was taking master's classes in an Organizational Leadership program and began meeting with one of my favorite professors, Ray Rood, for coffee once a month. I've mentioned Ray before in other books, as my time with him was so pivotal, but the power of Ray Rood can be summed up in his personal motto that he gives himself permission to give other people permission to be themselves. Ray is one of those special sages who is so secure in his own skin that he is able to create a space for you to breathe and blossom.

So as my working world is tossing me from one wave to another, these one-hour meetings with Ray outside a donut shop at 6:30 a.m. became my refuge from the storm.

Ray took me through a process he created called Strategic Futuring, telling me time and time again that "the future belongs to those who dare to envision the future, treat their vision as fact, and take responsibility for translating their vision into reality."

Ray was teaching me how to treat hope, and my hope in my future, as a fact. The Strategic Futuring process consists of many steps, culminating in writing out a vision for your life twenty years from now, in first person, as if you're living it. So as I'm just married, having been rejected by all the publishers, now working in a cubicle, and sitting outside during my lunch break in the sweltering heat and smog of southern California, I'm writing out a day in my life twenty years from now, fighting through the doubts and fears of what's "realistic." I hear Ray's encouragement in my head as I write: "You can't realistically plan twenty years out. So just dream and let go. Don't worry about if it's realistic or not."

My present felt so dim, yet here I was trying to write about this amazingly bright future where I'd be getting up to kids in the morning, in Colorado, working for myself as a successful author, etc. I tried not to let the lies write the day for me, but what I felt inside was the truth. I was fighting to treat the hope of my future as fact.

Well, it's been ten years now since I wrote out that twenty-year vision. And I just wrote Ray an email telling him that almost everything about that vision I wrote has come true. It is my life, except I stumbled onto most of it in ten years, not twenty! I thought I was dreaming ridiculously big. Turns out, it wasn't nearly big enough.

Just like Andy Dufresne in *Shawshank Redemption*. Who saw the vision of himself restoring a boat on a beach and worked every night, digging a tunnel with a tiny rock hammer.

As his best friend Red explained: "I remembering thinking it would take a man six hundred years to dig through the walls. Old Andy did it in less than twenty." [5]

Hope of redemption and freedom is what kept Andy digging at night. His escape tunnel was his own prison side hustle. **Hope and hard work are a powerful combo.**

Yet, it's Red, who once argued with Andy that hope was a dangerous thing, who is now riding on a bus after being released from prison as he begins his journey to hopefully find Andy, and then realizes that Andy was right about hope all along.

"I find I'm so excited I can barely sit still or hold a thought in my head. I think it's the excitement only a free man can feel. A free man at the start of a long journey whose conclusion is uncertain."

As the camera pans over the beautiful Pacific Ocean and Red finds his friend Andy on the beach, the two friends embrace. The last words of this painful, redemptive, harrowing movie come out of Red's mouth . . . "I hope . . ."

Hope is a powerful thing. And even when things don't feel very hopeful in our twenties, we can hope. We must cling to hope as a fact, not a fleeting feeling. Hope is a lifeboat when your ship is sinking, not the mirage of some island that will never come. Sure, it would've been better if the ship didn't sink at all, but gosh, when you're climbing into a small boat that's going to keep you afloat, that's better than spending a few nights in the dark ocean.

When we lose hope, we lose. We lose that ability to break away from a ho-hum, half-lived life because we start believing this is the best we can do. Hope is what keeps us from being "institutionalized"—it keeps us trying for more because we believe that more awaits. When we lose that belief, we are in danger.

We can become so confused in our twenties, so sure we've missed our chance, and in that confusion we are certain our life is over. How does this make sense?

We are so quick to say our future is over when we have so much future left to live. Your future takes time. Keep the hope alive.

The Power of Hope

I don't want to live institutionalized in my own personal prison, losing hope that things will never change. The hope of a better life is the only thing that kept Andy Dufresne and Red alive. There are so many times in our twenties, and in the many years thereafter, where it can feel like we will never escape the current situation we are in. I'm here to tell you, we will. Things will change. They always do.

When things in our life look grim, what if we chose to embrace the excitement of the uncertain instead of being afraid of it. It's like living out that powerful image of Andy in *Shawshank Redemption* where he's just climbed through a 500-yard sewer pipe and has escaped prison right into a thunderstorm. He doesn't run for cover from the pouring rain and the lighting crashing all around. He reaches his hands up to the sky and soaks it all in.

Hope gives us the ability to be at peace when the world around us is whipped up in an anxious frenzy. To believe in our future even when we don't know what our next step is. To explore. To see. To believe. To hope.

To always hope.

NEXT STEPS:

- **Hope lived as fact and hard work are a powerful combo.**

- Do you treat hope more as a feeling or a fact? Does hope seem naïve or is hope a necessity?

- *Shawshank Redemption* can be a tough movie to watch—one that I wouldn't recommend to everyone—but if you've seen it before, try rewatching it through the lens of hopelessness versus hope. How does that change the meaning of the movie to you?

- Is hope something that ebbs and flows depending on the details of your day, or is your hope tied to something more permanent and rooted? It's only when our source of hope goes deep that we are able to drink from its wells, even on dry, scorching days (and years!).

- There's nothing more certain in your twenties than uncertainty. Of this I'm certain. And I write this statement while sitting in a world of uncertainty during the quarantine of COVID-19. So I have no idea what the world looks like when this book is making it into your hands. But as I sit in a literal world of unknowns, I choose hope over the headlines. I sit and feel the uncertainty, then I make a conscious choice to choose hope and keep working hard toward my future. Don't make all the headlines become your headline. Choose hope over fear. Don't let uncertainty overwhelm you. Overwhelm it with hope.

- How do we do that? Choose to listen to people who promote life over fear. Choose to turn off the divisiveness playing out on social media most nights and go for a walk instead. Pray, if you're so inclined, and see what happens. Ask God for peace and wisdom. Choose to believe you have a future even when your reality feels futureless. War for hope. Every day.

LIE #5

None of this matters

What men daily do, not knowing what they do!

—William Shakespeare,
Much Ado About Nothing

Have you ever watched the *Chef's Table* series on Netflix? It's one of my favorites. There's an episode on the Roca brothers, three Italian brothers who run a top Michelin-starred restaurant. The episode focuses on the youngest brother, Jordi, who has become one of the most amazing and inventive pastry chefs in the world. But in his twenties, Jordi came close to ruining any chance he had. His brothers were much older than him, and they had already been working for years creating a top restaurant.

Yet Jordi was unsure if this was the industry he wanted to work in, so they hired him to bus tables. But Jordi felt like the outcast of the family, and he worked just enough that he could have some money to party afterward. So much so, that he asked to be transferred into the kitchen because the kitchen staff got off thirty minutes earlier than the servers, leaving him time to party more.

None of the work mattered to him. It wasn't the work he wanted to do, so he didn't work very hard. And of course, his brothers noticed, causing a deeper rift in the family and leaving the brothers with no choice but to think about firing their own brother.

Since Jordi didn't enjoy the work, he didn't think it mattered if he actually did the work. But of course it mattered. It mattered greatly to his brothers, who were trying to run a business. But it would matter to Jordi in the full scope of his life, even though he didn't realize it at that time. Because in his indifference, he was slowly killing his relationships and himself. He couldn't see the future, so he acted like the present didn't matter. In doing so, he almost missed his calling.

His brothers gave him one last chance, and instead of firing him, they gave him to the pastry chef to work on the desserts. There, Jordi began slowly seeing what his brothers saw about a life in the restaurant, and he started enjoying it. And only when the top pastry chef, who also liked to stay out late partying, broke his legs and couldn't return to work, was Jordi thrust into a sink-or-swim position as the only person in charge. And there Jordi slowly and painfully, with lots of mistakes in between, worked on his craft and realized his calling. Today, he's one of the best pastry chefs in the world.

You see, what you're doing right now, regardless of the situation, it matters.

It matters to your character. It matters to your skill set. It matters to your relationships. It matters to your growth. It matters to the people you're going to need to help in the future.

Indifference is a choice. You lose a lot when you lie to yourself that it doesn't matter what you lose.

I think we all have to fight against this lie—especially when we feel lost, confused, or hopeless.

When you're lost in the woods, each step actually matters much more than when you know exactly where you're going.

So when you're working in a lousy job, well, what does it matter if you work hard or not? No one will notice one way or another.

Your relationship with your significant other is going through a rocky season and they just hurt you. *What does it matter if I start flirting with that person at the coffee shop? What does it matter if I take out my ex for a drink? My significant other hurt me first.*

No matter the circumstances that led you there, you can't become careless in your confusion.

When you do that, there are always consequences. When you lose that sense of significance in the small things you are doing, how will you ever find the big, important things?

You need to become even more careful when you are the most confused.

Same is true when you feel lost, hopeless, or hurt. The worst thing you can do is think, *Well, none of this matters*, and start thrashing around in the dense fog. The worst thing you can do in the dark is start running full speed.

When you find yourself lost in the dark, that's the time to slow down the most. To really focus on your other senses, you have to force yourself to think clearly and critically. It's when you panic and try to frantically escape that you end up becoming more lost or hurting yourself and others.

The steps you take in the dark matter the most, because that is when you have the least margin for error. Each step has the possibility to lead to your rescue or to becoming more lost.

Sometimes you just have to sit down in the dark and ask for help. Sometimes (most times) you can't see the full path ahead. But that doesn't mean that each step doesn't matter. Each step is taking you somewhere. Is it around in circles or is it toward your future? Each step, each job, and each relationship matters, greatly.

Indifference is a lie that is trying to cover up fear and insecurity. If I don't really try, then I can never really fail. I'll always have a good excuse about why I'm never really doing anything worthwhile.

I'll continue to ridicule everyone who is putting themselves out there as my way of continuing to hide.

Yet, Nobel laureate Elie Wiesel experienced the greatest evil of indifference the world has ever seen from a nation that pretended

47

the concentration camps of WWII in Nazi Germany were not really happening. He doesn't let indifference just mildly walk away:

> The opposite of love is not hate, it's indifference. The opposite of art is not ugliness, it's indifference. The opposite of faith is not heresy, it's indifference. And the opposite of life is not death, it's indifference.[1]

Too many of us in this culture are indifferent to our indifference. We refuse to take a stand on anything as we continue to feel crushed by everything.

Taking action does not mean watching people talk about taking action on TV. Watching infotainment on Fox News or CNN is like being hungry and trying to fill yourself up on white bread. It takes away the pangs of hunger, while leaving you worse off than before. Or as Robert D. Putnam put it in *Bowling Alone*, "TV-based politics is to political action as watching *ER* is to saving someone in distress."[2]

Or most times we do nothing about a problem because we think someone else will do it. In psych theory this is called the Bystander Effect.

What does it matter if I do something or not about this problem because someone smarter, more capable, more financially secure will do something about it. You know, like a friend we'll call Andrew. He is better spoken than me and he understands the problem more clearly. If I got involved, I will just get in the way of the work Andrew is going to do on the matter.

And maybe Andrew is all those things. But do you know what Andrew is thinking? Kelsi, she's the one to meet this problem head-on. She's smarter and a better researcher than me. Plus, people follow her. Me? I'm just a nerdy introvert.

We pass responsibility down the line to the next person, never realizing that we're standing in a circle, playing a game of indifference like it's duck-duck-goose. Each of us tagging the person to the left and right, just to run around the circle and sit right back in the same place we started.

Do something. Do anything. Small. Big. In the spotlight. In the shadow. You will never make a difference if you're living a life of indifference.

None of this really matters is the excuse that fear tries to force on us. Don't let it. The lousy job you're working at does matter. What your parents and mentors are trying to talk to you about right now does matter. The relationship you're working through right now does matter. The mundane matters. It all matters.

If you never want to be critiqued, never try anything. Yet, what will people say after you've breathed your last breath? What will the final critique of your life be? Will people be talking about the scathing burns you gave out on Twitter or will they be talking about the difference you made?

When I die, I don't want people talking about what I critiqued; I want them talking about what I created.

I want my life, and your life, to matter. How will we be able to do that if we keep lying to ourselves that none of this matters?

NEXT STEPS:

- Can you spot any excuses you make for not doing the work you know you need to be doing? Being intentional and doing good work should not be based on our circumstances. As I first wrote in *101 Secrets for Your Twenties*, sometimes "we can learn the most in the jobs we like the least."[3]

- What kind of things can you be learning right now, even if your working or living situation is not ideal? In my own life, like in Jordi's, I think I worked for a few years longer in jobs I didn't really enjoy because I didn't always give my job the best. So it took me longer to learn what I needed to learn there.

- Can you spot any fears or insecurities that are holding you back from taking steps toward pursuing something you know you should be pursuing? Can you spot any ways you are escaping from reality rather than facing it head-on and doing something to change it? Write down a few of these ideas.

LIE #6

Love is all you need

The Beatles might have led us wrong on this one. Before you send me some Beatles hate mail, let me explain.

Love is amazing. We love talking, singing, and writing about love. We love love. But what exactly are we loving so much about love?

I think in our relationships, we need to stop using "love" as the litmus test.

I've got nothing against love. Or saying "I love you." My wife and I say that to each other all the time.

But what do we really mean when we tell our significant other or our hopefully significant other, or even our friend or family member, that we love them? What are we really saying? Is it different when you tell your significant other you love them than it is when you tell your parent or your schnoodle puppy?

Love is very complicated. Love can be a liar and love can tell the cold, hard truth. Love is complex—it can bring more confusion or it can bring clarity.

If we're saying all we need is love, we'd better understand the totality of that statement. And if all we need is love, why are so many people who were *in* love and got married, falling *out* of love and getting divorced?

The Power of Love

Oftentimes we treat love as if it's this alien that has abducted our body. We are powerless to fight against it. Sometimes we make very bad decisions to stay in very bad relationships under the banner of "*But . . . I love them . . .*"

Sometimes the feelings of love blind us to the facts of dysfunction. That's not exactly Valentine's card material, but that's the unlovely truth of it.

Even the way we describe love is interesting. We often describe love as a fall. So is love a big crack in the sidewalk that we trip on? We plummet. Whether our fall ends on a soft, billowy mattress or on rocky cement seems out of our control. Because, like gravity, we cannot escape its pull.

I'm falling in love. So does that mean if you fall in, you can quickly fall out? Does that mean you've lost all control and are dangerously picking up speed as you rapidly cascade toward some extremely hard landing after the fall? You can't fall in perpetuity. At some point that falling has to stop. And if you're not falling anymore, are you in love?

Whether the end result of our love is more a Hallmark Christmas movie starring the ever-adorable Candace Cameron Bure or a Shakespearean play where everyone dies doesn't actually seem all that important to us. Because we are falling in love. Sure, this person has more red flags waving at us than a Russian parade. Sure, they cheated on us. Lied to us. Revealed to us behind closed doors their true colors that actually look nothing like the colors that show out in the light, but *what can I do about it? I love them.* I've been abducted. The alien has taken over my body. I must do as it says.

The Greeks Loved Love Too

The Greeks had all kinds of different words for love because they knew there are many different kinds and shapes of love.

Eros is often the love we describe in romantic relationships. It is the passionate, steamy love that we often view as the pinnacle of a relationship. It is the intense feeling of love.

While feelings of love aren't necessarily bad, when eros is the only driver of the bus, it might end up less like a romantic road trip and more like the movie *Speed* where you feel like you can't slow down lest the ticking time bomb explodes. Yet, that becomes the biggest bomb of all. Then next thing you know, *Speed 2* comes around, and Keanu Reeves and Sandra Bullock are breaking up because the ticking excitement and intensity of eros love has ticked out.

Then there's love like *agape* and *philia* that might hold more of the cornerstones to a healthy relationship. Love that is altruistic, giving, sacrificial, and wants what's best for the other. Yet, if you're obsessively *agaping* a relationship and they are doing nothing of the sort, your love will feel completely lopsided, like a teeter-totter that doesn't teeter.

Let's jump out of ancient Greece and jump into today's world. What if we look at "I love you" through some different lenses? What does that do to your view of love?

Different Ways to Say "I Love You"

What if there are better ways to say "I love you" than by saying "I love you"?

How about . . .

I trust you. Trust is hard to make-believe. You can play house with feelings of love. It's really hard to start a home with someone you don't trust.

Trust is there or it's not. It takes time to build and a moment to explode. If you're thinking of marrying someone, you are trusting them with your life. And they are trusting their life with you. It's as visual and extreme as stepping onto a battlefield with someone.

When the bullets start flying, you better trust that person next to you is going to stay. Is going to have your back. Is not going to turn their gun toward you and start shooting out of panic and fear.

When you trust the person next to you, you're going to fight against everything that's trying to get you fighting. You have to depend on this person. With your life. When tragedy strikes. With all the mundane, non-sexy adult life details like paying bills, cleaning the house, making money, and working off debt.

And if you're thinking of having kids someday, or you do have kids, would you trust this person to take care of them when you're not around? If this thought makes you squirm, it might be a neon sign that trust isn't very visible.

Sidenote on trust: It's also going to be really hard to trust someone if you don't trust yourself. Because your internal unrest is going to spew like a geyser at inopportune times. How do you build a house on that? How can trust be a bedrock in your relationship when it's spinning around like a Tilt-a-Whirl inside your own mind and heart?

If you can't depend on who you are, it's going to be hard to have a healthy interdependence on someone else.

Trust is best formed when two people working toward wholeness come together to fill the spaces in between.

Love can feel mysterious. Trust is blunt. Love is like a flamboyant tango instructor showing you the sexy and the sizzle. Trust is like your accountant showing you the stark reality of your financial statements. The numbers don't lie.

Trust doesn't lie.

It's really hard to build a life with someone when trust is not the cement you're pouring in between the cracks. Sure, you think you love them. But do you know you trust them?

I might love flying to Hawaii, but if I spot the pilot beforehand and he's clearly five mai tais north of sober, my love for beaches isn't going to be enough for me to trust the pilot with my life 35,000 feet up in the air.

I value and respect you. When you can honestly say this about someone, it shows you have some shared values with them. Typically, what we value in someone else is what we aspire to live out in our own lives.

If shared values are present, then trust will be close behind. For my wife and me, as I look back on our relationship after fifteen years and four kids together, it was those shared values that kept us afloat during seasons of choppy water. We both knew our values and they aligned with each other, in regard to our faith and the vision we had for our lives. Our shared values gave our relationship a compass to navigate from and built-in mutual respect.

Shared values are an amazing safety net. Something you will continue to fall back on in your relationship.

Trust is the skeleton of your relationship. Shared values are the red blood cells carrying oxygen throughout.

I will sacrifice for you. We act like telling someone you love them is ultimate. How about telling someone you'll sacrifice for them? You don't exactly hear *The Bachelor* contestants running to say this.

Sacrifice means you're giving up something important to you. Your time. Space. Freedom to do whatever you want whenever you want. Personal comfort. Your favorite TV show on Thursday nights. It's not a sacrifice if it first wasn't important to you.

A relationship is all a dance of give-and-take, especially if kids come into the picture. Then you realize how selfish you really are. Because kids need a lot from parents, and if you're the only one willing to sacrifice, then your kids will become a weight that is tough to carry by yourself.

I believe in you. A little different than trust, saying you believe in someone is telling them you think they have what it takes. You think they can obtain the vision they see for the future. Believing in someone is peeking behind the curtain and not being scared by a lack of substance there but actually liking what you see. You see their skills, character, values, and habits, and you're saying, "Sign me up for that ride of a lifetime."

If my wife, Naomi, didn't believe in me, I never would've published a book. When every publisher was turning me down, she saw something in me that I stopped seeing about ten rejections ago. She believed in me, and it was her belief that gave me the space and grace to fail and struggle for years before that first book deal.

In turn, as she transitioned from college admissions counselor to financial adviser, I believed she could do it. We both knew it wasn't going to be easy. It would involve sacrifice from both of us. But I believed she had the ability and perseverance to make it happen. And she did—the only person out of her training program who made it through the Great Recession as she won awards for best Junior adviser.

It's really hard to manufacture trust and respect when secretly you don't believe in that person. When life's paths get dark and confusing, infatuation is not a very bright light.

I enjoy spending time with you. It still amazes me how many people say they love each other, and yet they don't want to spend more than five minutes together. Marriage, you know, kind of takes a lot of time. If you need an epic Costa Rican vacation to enjoy spending time with each other, then the other 99.9 percent of the time might be a little sketchy. I've said it before, but marriage is much more mundane than magical.

All You Need Is Love?

All you need is love and a lot of other things that make love, love.

If you're struggling with defining your love for someone, can you honestly make these other statements instead?

Besides all of this, understand that a great relationship will only complement you, never complete you. If this one person is the answer you're looking for, you're asking the wrong question. No matter how amazing this person is or how many boxes your relationship checks. If you are looking for any one person to complete you, you are going to be an incomplete mess for years to come. They will let you down. You will let them down.

But if your relationship is built on trust, respect, values, belief—well, then your relationship will be built on a lot more fact than fiction. You won't complete each other, but you'll help each other refine some of the incompleteness.

NEXT STEPS:

- Can you honestly make these other statements about someone you love? If not, why not? What is that saying about you and that relationship?

- Sometimes, especially in regard to a past friend or a current family member, you can love someone deeply, yet you don't want to spend time with them. You've come to grips with the fact that a healthy relationship is not possible with them, so while you want what's best for them, you know that it can include only short interactions with them in your life. You love them, but you don't trust them.

- Trust, respect, belief, shared values, time, and sacrifice. If these words honestly aren't a big part of your relationship, then what is your love built on? Whether you're single or in a relationship, it's time to sit down and define what a healthy, thriving relationship looks and feels like to you. Ask yourself, or sit down with your significant other, and start putting definitions down as to what trust, values, respect, sacrifice, belief, and quality time look like to you. Define these before the overwhelming feelings of love define these for you.

LIE #7

I better get mine

Los Angeles is the place where grand dreams go to die.

Maybe that's a bit of an overstatement. But if you've ever tried to get a job of any kind in Hollywood, or just driven for one hour on an LA freeway, you know that there should be a class action lawsuit for false advertising against LA's motto "City of Angels." There are not many rosy-cheeked cherub angels playing harps as they scoot around on clouds on the 405 freeway.

No, merging onto any LA freeway is like entering into a war zone. You fight for every rotation of your tires. The biggest mistake you can make on an LA freeway? Using your blinker. That just signals the person behind you to speed up and make sure the lane change does not happen in front of them. No matter what. They've been fighting for an hour to get to this place, and they are not about to let a happy, blinker-using Prius enter into their territory.

In LA if you need to change lanes, you spot that gap and swerve over without warning. Then, once firmly established in the lane, you turn on your blinker to let the person in back of you know, "Yeah, that just happened."

But it's not just LA life that is this way. As the Lumineers sing, "Living life in the city will never be pretty." Anytime you have too many people trying to cram into too small of an area, there's bound to be some tension as people "fight" for what is theirs.

One afternoon, after battling for an hour on an LA freeway to drive seven miles, I somehow still made it five minutes before my upcoming meeting was scheduled to start. You learn quickly in LA that if you really need to get somewhere on time, there's no such thing as leaving too early.

I was in some port—an industrial city on the West Coast—and as I started walking, I took a minute to collect myself as I leaned against a rail and looked at a beach by the ocean.

This was not the kind of beach a resort was going to put on the front of their brochure. With all the trash that littered the area, taking a dip in the water would pretty much be jumping straight into the loving arms of an infectious disease.

No one in sight, the only living creatures I could see were a group of seagulls. And if I'd come to this spot overlooking the ocean, searching for peace and silence after my insane drive down the 405 freeway, the unsightly trash heap on the beach and the circling seagulls were not about to let me find it.

Twenty seagulls shrieked and fought, dive-bombing each other as each one fought to get a piece of trash. I was witnessing a Seagull Battle to the Death as they bit and fought to get a scrap far enough from the masses so that they could eat.

I watched this spectacle for minutes, when I started laughing. The ridiculousness of the situation hit me. These seagulls are fighting each other to the death for a bite of trash, and here we are at an ocean abundant with food and resources galore!

That's when I noticed the one seagull that was floating in the water. Calm. Quiet. He'd already realized that truth before I did. And as the seagulls screeched, he ebbed and flowed in peaceful waters. The one seagull that knew something the others didn't.

Years later, this image keeps coming back to me. And I fear, all too often, I am one of those screeching seagulls. A whole world of opportunities, resources, and adventure right there in front of me, yet I choose to fight over the easy bite, even if it is trash.

Why do the seagulls go for the trash? Well, it's there, and looks easy to grab. But there's a limited amount, so a fight ensues! In the summer when the beach is littered in pizza boxes and candy wrappers, the seagulls go a little crazy. You open a bag of Cheetos and throw it in the air, and you better watch out for the seagulls going full "Spring Breakers in Miami" mode, fighting each other for just one flaming hot Cheeto like it's the last scrap of something edible on earth.

How many days do I live the same way? Out of fear, I don't want to explore. The adventure in front of me is not inviting, it's overwhelming. I don't see the possibilities; I see the danger of the unknowns. So I go for the low-hanging fiery Cheeto instead of something substantial and life giving.

The (In)Sane Society

German Jewish psychologist Erich Fromm argues in *The Sane Society*:

> The danger of the future is that men may become robots. . . . But given man's nature, robots cannot live and remain sane, they become "Golems," they will destroy their world and themselves because they cannot stand any longer the boredom of a meaningless life.[1]

I fear this warning above plays out all too often in today's world. We see way too many "Golems" fighting each other, robotically spouting the party lines and trying to crush anyone who disagrees. But how much of the vileness toward each other comes not from hate but from boredom. From a bunch of people fighting over scraps because they don't feel like they have hope for anything better.

Lost hope is a dangerous thing. Believing that *this* is the best there is can be a scary thought.

Yet, I far too often live the same way. I complain and mumble and get wrapped up in fighting wars that really aren't mine to fight. I complain that my cubicle walls are closing in on me, but if I'm being honest with myself, there were many years I was too scared to leave them. We complain about bosses because that's much easier to do than being your own. We complain about systems and structures but are much too overwhelmed to try and create better ones. We say we want freedom, but when we get it, we yearn to go right back to the comfort of captivity.

I'm reminded again of the classic movie *Shawshank Redemption* where some of the prisoners argue that if you stay in the prison too long, you become "institutionalized," like longtime prisoner Brooks. The prison walls are harsh, unloving, yet they are known. So we stay. We want to change. We need to change. But we're scared to change. The thing we want to escape from the most becomes the thing that feels the most inescapable. But in our case, the prison door is open and we're choosing to stay inside. Fear is our prison guard.

When we fail to explore and risk out of fear, we fight over the scraps. We willingly become cogs. We become prisoners stuck in wide-open prison cells.

We start living with a mindset of "I better get mine," as we fail to see the abundance that is a little farther out on the horizon. We screech, and bite, and dive-bomb, and quarrel because we're bored, while also being afraid. We're living just to survive. We don't think we can do better, so we fight over the trash.

Modern man still is anxious and tempted to surrender his freedom to dictators of all kinds, or to lose it by transforming himself into a small cog in the machine, well fed, and well clothed, yet not a free man but an automaton.
—Erich Fromm

I'm referencing all facets of our lives here—our careers, callings, friendships, impact, and all-around place in this world. When we start fighting over the scraps, we lose vision of the future. When we keep worrying about what everybody else is getting, we fail to see all the gifts waiting there right in front of us. When we are constantly fighting for "what is ours," we lose sight of all that is waiting for us . . . an abundance of life.

Life Lived in the Ocean

I see that seagull calmly floating in the water looking for a fresh fish, and I imagine him with a slight smirk on his face as he watches his friends fight over trash. If only they could see what he sees, he thinks. If only they could remember what they should already know. That abundance awaits them, but they have to be willing to look for it. To work for it.

As C. S. Lewis poignantly described: "We are half-hearted creatures, fooling about with drink and sex and ambition when infinite joy is offered us, like an ignorant child who wants to go on making mud pies in a slum because he cannot imagine what is meant by the offer of a holiday at sea. We are far too easily pleased."[2]

Even the seagulls know when they need to get serious. When the seagulls are going to lay eggs and have babies, they say goodbye to the half-eaten Twinkie and they start working again.

They know when enough is enough and they need to actually find the nourishing stuff that wasn't conjured up in a factory. Fish. Bugs. Crabs. Small reptiles. Seagulls know when it's time to get serious and go for substance. Do we?

I don't want to fight over the scraps when a world of abundance is waiting right there in front of me. This is not only good advice on how to live our lives but also sound business strategy explained in the book, aptly titled, *Blue Ocean Strategy*. I'm wondering if the authors watched the battle of the seagulls as well.

The basic premise of *Blue Ocean Strategy* is for companies not to compete over the scraps but to find nuanced, strategic ideas that move so far into the ocean they are no longer competing with the seagulls. They use examples like Cirque du Soleil, who turned the circus into something far different and far beyond the big-tent tops of Barnum and Bailey, and created its own successful Blue Ocean. Or Yellowtail wine, which turned the snobbery of the wine industry on its head and created affordable wines for the everyday person.[3] Companies that are fighting over the same pile of scraps are companies that will struggle to thrive.

Same for us.

I don't want to live as a well-fed, well-clothed cog. Where if I quit or am fired, they will simply put another cog into the machine and I won't be missed for a day.

I don't want to live a bored and meaningless life, fighting over a half-eaten bag of sandy, flamin' hot Cheetos when an ocean awaits in front of me.

I want to live in the Blue Ocean, seeing the needs and resources that are in front of me, and using my skills, values, and strengths to swim out and live abundantly. Give abundantly. Be abundant.

How about you?

NEXT STEPS:

- When we fail to explore and risk out of fear, we fight over the scraps. Can you spot any ways that you are fighting over the scraps with the rest of the seagulls and need to escape the fight?
- Can you see any Blue Oceans in front of you? Needs, problems, or frustrations that you've been complaining about or frustrated with that you can help fix?

LIE #8

I deserve to be happy

Happiness is overrated.

—Brad Pitt

We hear the phrase "I deserve to be happy" thrown around a lot these days. And it's a tricky one. Even mentioning that it might be more lie than truth I'm guessing has some readers ready to pick up their pitchforks and come after me.

Yet, here's what I think is the truth: The more we pursue happiness, the less happy we're going to be.

Now hear me out, I'm all for people being happy. I don't want to have the countenance of an emo rockstar, writing a song while sitting on a jagged rock in the pouring rain.

But what are we really saying when we say, "I deserve to be happy"? I don't think this belief is the pathway to happiness. I think it actually might make us more unhappy than when we started. Problem is, when we start living by "I deserve to be happy," we start making some decisions that make us more unhappy than before. "I deserve to be happy!" becomes a code phrase for "I'm about to make some really bad life choices, but I don't want anyone calling me on them!"

First, What Is Happiness?

Is happiness the product? Or is happiness a by-product of something else? Can we seek happiness unto itself? Or is happiness a natural by-product when we're pursuing something else meaningful?

For all of us, when we're unhappy with our lives, we can too easily pursue a quick, counterfeit happiness that leaves us feeling worse off than before. Maybe a spending spree becomes that answer to unhappiness for you. Or abusing some substance that always leaves you feeling worse yet wanting more. Or getting back into an unhealthy relationship that made you very unhappy, but at this specific moment of unhappiness, it suddenly becomes the logical, illogical answer to filling that void.

We don't end up finding happiness; we merely find a distraction from our unhappiness. I still see this play out in my own life way too many times. Do you?

Seeking happiness to be happy is like smoking a cigarette to soothe your anxiety. Its effects are fleeting. It's a quick fix. You constantly need more. There's never that one magical cigarette that you smoke where you sit back and think, "Man, that one did it. That's going to tide me over for at least the next five years."

Smoking a cigarette to give you peace is a never-ending cycle that kills you way more than it makes you whole.

UC Berkeley psychologist Iris Mauss and fellow researcher Maya Tamir of Hebrew University, as cited by Berkeley news, found that people who placed a higher premium on happiness reported higher rates of stress, discontentment, and even depression than those who did not set a happiness goal. The results suggest that the proverbial pursuit of happiness can actually heighten awareness of how one is falling short of that goal.[1]

As we pursue happiness, we will constantly be aware of all the ways we are unhappy.

> Many persons have a wrong idea of what constitutes true happiness. It is not attained through self-gratification but through fidelity to a worthy purpose.
>
> —Helen Keller

Time and time again, we see that feelings of happiness, contentment, and joy are by-products of serving others and being committed to something bigger than ourselves.

Yet, you don't see a lot of people on Twitter shouting, "I deserve to be happy! So I don't care what anyone says, I'm going to that soup kitchen today to feed the homeless!"

No, it's usually "I just spent $3,000 to go to the Fyre Festival! It's a private island that used to be owned by Pablo Escobar! Bands, booze, bougieness to the extreme. I know it's a lot of money, but I deserve to be happy!!!"

The results of the Fyre Festival is a fitting metaphor for that pursuit of happiness (just watch one of the Fyre Festival documentaries). When we pursue this kind of happiness, it's not "cake by the ocean" but a cafeteria cheese sandwich in a disaster relief tent. Shouting "I deserve to be happy" usually precedes a pretty unhealthy and unwise disaster that leaves you more unhappy than when you started.

Marriage and Happiness

If you go into a marriage holding on to this belief that you deserve to be happy no matter what, then sadly I can almost guarantee you a very unhappy marriage.

Because feelings of love ebb and flow. Because a solid marriage is built on both sides making sacrifices for the well-being of the other and of the relationship. Self-seeking and sacrifice don't play nice together.

66

A self-seeking marriage won't be much of a marriage, because at some point, it will not serve you and your happiness like you think it should.

I want you to know your deep worth and purpose. You have a deep inherent worth. You have great value. You have so much substance. But if you're just pursuing happiness, what are you really going to be pursuing? What kind of life will that lead to?

Sometimes this pursuit of happiness comes under the guise of self-care. Again, as I hope you're able to see throughout this book, I'm all about *a whole, healthy, meaningful life*. So with that said, I do think we need to be careful that our "self-care" doesn't become self-destructive self-indulgence. If your self-care is putting you thousands in debt, how is that helping yourself? If your self-care is consistently alienating your loved ones, how is that caring for yourself and others?

And I say this next part as someone who cares for you like your brother, wanting you to live your best life. If your pursuit of "happiness" is pushing you deeper into some dark holes next to some dark people affixed to some dark addictions, then you need to quickly escape this pursuit of happiness. I implore you to stop abusing the substances that kill your substance.

If your "I deserve to be happy" has you waking up in some strange places with some strange, disturbing memories that you would never tell your mother about, you *deserve* something much greater than this.

Let's stop pursuing happiness to be happy. Happiness, unto itself, is overrated. It promises a lot and delivers very little.

Instead, let's pursue meaning. Pursue purpose. Pursue wisdom and truth. Pursue doing good work. Pursue loving others well. Pursue making and creating something beautiful and life-giving. Pursue spiritual, emotional, mental, and physical health. Then I promise joy and contentment will flow more naturally from this consistent spring of life than from the dried-up creek of happiness

> I began learning long ago that those who are happiest are those who do the most for others.
>
> —Booker T. Washington

that you keep trying to fill up with a garden hose. Let joy come from a deep well of substance and meaning, not from your next hit of happiness.

Happiness is lemonade. It's refreshing. It's sugary. It gives you a quick rush. Yet, if you drink only lemonade and never drink plain old boring water, then you're going to be sick.

Let's strive to be healthy and whole. Let's pursue purpose and meaning. Let's seek a deep, rich life, not a shallow, hollow one. Serve others. Create and make. Let's be a part of something bigger than ourselves.

Happiness is the most apparent in my life when I'm not seeking it.

Stop pursuing happiness and watch yourself be more happy. Give it a try. It might make you happier than you ever could've imagined.

I do want you to be happy. So stop pursuing it.

NEXT STEPS:

- If happiness is the sole focus of your life, it becomes even more difficult to be happy. Happiness is a by-product of something more meaningful, not the product itself. Self-indulgence is not the pathway to sustainable happiness.

- Can you spot any patterns in your life where you can see you've been pursuing an immediate fix, more of a distraction *away* from unhappiness rather than a substantial joy?

- Can you spot other parts of your life where you are pursuing something that consistently makes you feel more healthy and whole as a by-product because it is rooted in purpose and meaning?

LIE #9

Everyone is doing better than me

You quickly scan the lines at the grocery store. You wanted to get there before the rush-hour crowd, but since you had to drive through rush hour in your attempt to beat rush hour, your timing wasn't exactly on point. Now all of downtown is jammed into two food aisles, also trying to figure out what the heck to make for dinner tonight.

Somehow you grab some food, then rush up front to see that the checkout lines now look like Disneyland. Except when you finally get to the front of the line, there'll be no Splash Mountain waiting for you.

But, you know what, none of this is bothering you right now. You've just had a better-than-mediocre day at work. Your manager actually stopped and talked to you today, and even alluded to the fact that you're doing a good job and they're lucky to have you. Sure, they didn't say that, but you could read it in their eyes.

Then, you were stuck in rush hour, but it was in your brand-new car! Sure, you're just leasing it and you're hoping that if you don't think of the future payments, somehow they won't find you—like a baby covering their eyes to play peekaboo when you can see their whole body. But again, you're happy! And you just posted some pictures on social media of you celebrating your new car from all your hard work at your new job that you absolutely love. (Sure, you didn't mention the "just leasing" part and the fact that a "slightly better than mediocre day" at work is your gold standard, but these are just minor details.)

So while you're waiting for Splash Mountain, you jump on your phone to see how many likes your new car photo is getting! And it all comes crashing down. "Seven likes! That's it?!"

Okay, now you're pissed. You could take the mind-numbing day at work. You could take the rush-hour traffic. You can take the long line. You can take the elderly woman standing uncomfortably close to you as she tries to look at your phone. But seven likes for the photo of your new car that you couldn't wait to share? That's just too much!

So you start scrolling through everyone else's posts as your mood starts feeling like the kid's next to you, who is freaking out because his parents won't let him get that bag of gummy worms.

They got 107 likes of their sleeping baby? C'mon, they post a picture of the baby sleeping like every day! And it's not even cute. There, I said it.

143 likes about a guy's new social media marketing job! What? When I posted about my new job, I got barely anything.

She lost 14 pounds and gets 250 likes! Who wants to bet she gains it all back plus five pounds come Christmas.

343 likes! How in the world did she pull that off? Oh, she's clear of cancer. That's cool. I'll like that too. Maybe I should get a rare disease? That really seems to increase social media engagement. But I don't really want a rare disease. Maybe I fake it? Let me think more about that one.

By the time someone has to nudge you to tell you that you're at the front of the line, your mood has gone from "I can tackle anything adulthood throws at me" to "Let me down a whole gummy worm bag right in front of this little snot who was just throwing a tantrum for one—because 'Hey, look, kid, I'm an adult and I can do whatever the heck I want.'"

In one five-minute grocery line wait, you went from being a happy person, thankful for your blessings of the day, to an angry, bitter, judgmental person who is seriously contemplating a fake disease so you can get more very real fake social media validation. You go home, barely hanging on now to any sense of self-worth and motivation. You start making dinner when you realize the $57 worth of groceries you just bought don't come together in any way to actually make a meal.

Now, you're done.

It's Netflix, wine, and more gummy worms. That's your night. Drowning out your angst that came from social media while you watch Netflix while still, of course, continuing to scroll through more social media! More scrolling. More anger. More wine. More scrolling. More feelings of inadequacy. More bitterness. More wine. If this doesn't feel like the routine of champions, what does!

Really, does any one of us come away after being on social media for thirty minutes and think, "That was a great use of my time! Not only do I feel more energetic and ready to tackle my day, but I'm also now very thankful for this super loose connection of online friends who I never talk to, but now know every intricate detail of their life that I care nothing about, but can't seem to look away."

What if we treated other aspects of our life like we do social media?

"I'm so hungry and I've got lots of choices here in the kitchen . . . Oh wait, is that peanuts? You know, I had a handful of those little dickens yesterday, and you wouldn't believe the allergic reaction that cascaded down my throat like I tried to swallow 60-grit sandpaper. Sign me up, Mr. Peanuts! I'm ready for another dose. I'll just call an Uber for the hospital ahead of time, you know, in case I pass out before I can get to the phone."

Or . . .

"Oh, my old high school friend is inviting me out to the coffee shop. Last time we went out, all she did was talk about herself for an hour and half. Then she showed me 137 pictures of 137 days of her puppy sleeping. The only time she asked me a question was if I knew how many calories were in all that cream I was 'extravagantly' pouring into my coffee. Then she was nice enough to observe that my wardrobe could use a little 2020s, whatever that means. Which of course, led her to the real reason she invited me out—granting me the opportunity to personally be on the ground floor of the best 'yoga pants made from essential oils' multilevel marketing company that you'll ever want to quit three months from now. After of course you're down $1,550, but up seven sleek pairs of hot pink eucalyptus, oregano, lemongrass pants."

You didn't like doing homework as a kid, so you avoided doing it.

You didn't like vegetables, so you avoided eating them.

You don't like going on social media, but you spend the next three hours on it.

Just makes sense. At least homework and vegetables were actually good for you.

Social media has gone from being an exciting way to reconnect, to a hobby, to an obsession, to a chore you dread, to an addiction that you want to quit but can't quite figure out how.

Facebook: All the people I've personally avoided in my life are now the only people I'm talking to. *Please, just like my picture of my puppy and move along.*

Twitter: Look at all these memes! And horrible thoughts! And screaming at each other! And headlines about everything going to hell! I love it here!

Instagram: Look at their house! Look at their kids! Look at their car! Look at that bikini! Loooook!!!! How many filters do I need to layer on before I can be an Instagram influencer too!

TikTok: I'm starting to hit my limit here.

Whatever social media platform is popular when you're reading this: Hey, we have to connect there!

Social media has become that obligatory yearbook message you write at the end of the year. "We should totally hang out this summer! XOXOXO." (But please don't actually try and call me.)

Social media. You don't really want to be on it, yet you can't stop. You know how you'll feel afterward. Yet the pull is too strong. Now you're laid out on the couch with no motivation to move or think.

Isn't this kind of the telltale sign of an addiction? Like doing drugs or excessive alcohol. You don't want to do the thing you can't stop yourself from doing.

Obsessive Comparison Disorder

It's real and only becoming *realer* since I first wrote about it in 2012 on my website **allgroanup.com,** and then in my books *101 Secrets for Your Twenties* and *101 Questions You Need to Ask in Your Twenties.* I don't write about Obsessive Comparison Disorder to make light of Obsessive Compulsive Disorder and those who are struggling with it. I write about Obsessive Comparison Disorder to demonstrate the severity of our constant online comparison issue and what it's doing to us.

Obsessive Comparison Disorder is constantly letting everyone's "success" smother you like an electric blanket turned up on high in August. It doesn't work in moderation.

Obsessive Comparison Disorder. Like smoking, it's killing us at every swipe. We used to have to go to our ten-year reunion to see who's doing better than whom. Now, we're trying to fake our success with every post. Now we're paying $25 to go to the "Selfie Museum" downtown for us to post the most awesome fake photo (and yes, in case you were unaware, "Selfie Museums" are actual places in LA, Denver, and even in Iowa!).

But sometimes we're not even comparing our successes. We're comparing our hardships. Not who has it best, but who has it worst. Who has the biggest challenges? Who has the busiest, hardest, craziest circumstances that deserve the highest sympathies (and social media engagement)?

Or—and this is a strange one—we're obsessively comparing ourselves with *ourselves*. I didn't know this was possible either. But then you start scrolling through your own photos from a few years back. *Wow, look at how skinny I was! Look at how many friends I used to have! Look at me when I looked happy! Those shimmering eyes that thought they were going to change the world . . .*

Or we begin comparing a future image of ourselves that we thought we'd be, against the image we are currently looking at in the mirror. *I thought I'd be more successful by now. I thought I'd be married. I thought I'd have my stuff together. Instead, it feels like my stuff has somehow fallen out of the back of my car and I'm trying to pick it up off the highway as speeding cars barely avoid me.*

Obsessive Comparison Disorder is at the touch of our fingers. It's on us. In us. All around us. What is it doing to us?

Effects of Social Media on Our Mental State

Our Obsessive Comparison Disorder is creating isolation, anxiety, and depression. In a mental health and well-being article on social media and loneliness, author and therapist Sherry Amatenstein writes, "Frequently viewing curated snapshots of other people's lives might leave social media users feeling as if *everyone else has a better life, is smarter, funnier, more interesting, has more friends, etc.* The impulse to believe this illogical notion can be even stronger for social media users with low self-esteem."[1]

Demographically it seems young adults with heavy use of social media platforms—two hours a day—have twice the chance of experiencing social anxiety, according to a 2017 study.[2]

Author and professor of communication studies Gregory Spencer writes in *Reframing the Soul* about an ongoing conversation he has with the college students in his class:

> Why have appointments at the counseling center greatly increased? Why is suicide up? They are not researchers. They are just reporting what they experience as members of this group. One consistent answer is that they feel the weight of tremendous expectations. They make comparisons based on the perfect images they see on social media. They say, why don't I have as much fun, look as fantastic, go places as exotic? They feel the pressure of higher digital standards and the need to control their own images.[3]

Tim Cook, CEO of Apple since 2011, had this to say about social media: "I don't have a kid, but I have a nephew that I put some boundaries on. There are some things that I won't allow; I don't want him on a social network."[4]

The lie is "everyone is doing better than me." But here's the truth: the people who are probably doing better than all of us are the people who are never on social media documenting how much better they are doing than the rest.

The people who aren't addicted to the dopamine hit of another "like," the people who are doing good work and not needing to be validated in the process. Those people are probably doing better.

Everyone is struggling with something. Everyone has their *stuff*. Just because that fact is not being highlighted on social media doesn't mean it's not true.

NEXT STEPS:

- You can't judge a book by its cover. You can't judge a person by their pictures on social media.

- No one's life is as good as it looks on social media. Sometimes it's the lives that look the best on your feed that are in the biggest mess.

- Take a social media inventory of your life. Rank the social platforms from top to bottom, from the platform that adds the most to your life to the platform that seems to suck the most life out of you. Then seriously think about deleting or taking a break from the bottom few social media apps that are doing their best to make your life worse.

- If social media is doing nothing to improve your life, but only seems to bring you down into a pit of depression and anxiety, then maybe it's time to take a serious break from all of it. I've seen many people go on a social media "fast" for a period of time. If this doesn't seem possible, then at least put some parameters around the amount of time you spend on your phone. Look into the various apps or settings on the phone that will time you out if you're on your phone too long.

- Obsessive Comparison Disorder. Like smoking, it's killing us at every swipe. Let's stop it so it can no longer stop us.

LIE #10

I'm not good enough

There were two men who started pursuing a life in acting at the same time. As they trained in LA at the Pasadena Playhouse with a group of hopeful actors, they became close friends. They were both long shots to "make it." And if they needed proof of that fact, they both miraculously tied for an award at the end of the semester—"least likely to succeed."

They moved to New York and the younger of the two ended up sleeping on the older actor's kitchen floor. They hustled as much as they could, auditioning for every off-off-Broadway production they could find. They slid headshots under casting directors' doors, then ran away before they could be spotted.

As they struggled to break into the industry, they worked countless odd jobs to pay the bills. And the younger of the two worked some really odd, odd jobs during a decade of not making it. He waited tables, sure. But he also worked at a psychiatric hospital, as a sales assistant in Macy's toy department, sold hockey tickets, and even weaved Hawaiian garlands.

Yet, he had a different mindset than most twentysomethings as he worked these jobs. He treated each one as a role, a part. He treated each job as a chance to practice a persona. As he sold hockey game tickets, he donned a French Canadian accent so he could work on creating another believable character. Even though he felt like he was failing in his pursuit of acting, he wasn't calling himself a failure and giving up. When working these lousy jobs, a reality most twentysomethings can relate to, he brought purpose and intentionality to them by using them as tools to work on his craft. The lousy jobs had a purpose in working toward his dream job.

Finally, after years of slowly gaining more supporting roles on Broadway, he got his big chance at thirty years old to audition for a Hollywood film. The director of the movie had seen him in a play and wanted to give the no-name actor a shot. During the audition, the actor was so nervous he could feel his hands shaking and he was having trouble remembering his lines. For a day the director coached him and tried to make him feel at ease. But with the cameramen around and the bright lights in his face, he was having trouble concentrating. At the end of the audition, the actor recalled that "I went to shake the prop guy's hand and all my subway tokens fell out of my pocket. And he picked them up and handed them back to me saying, 'Here, kid, you're gonna need these.'"[1]

As he was fighting to get the biggest break of his career, he still had people trying to remind him he was never going to make it. Well, all those people were wrong, as they usually are.

So who is this actor and what big role was he auditioning for? Dustin Hoffman auditioning for the lead role of *The Graduate*.

Hoffman would get the role, starring in one of the most successful and iconic roles of his era. After shooting the film, that same prop director would give him a gift: a framed display of seven New York subway coins. It was the prop director's apology and way of saying Hoffman wasn't going to need those subway coins anymore.

After being voted least likely to succeed at the Pasadena Playhouse about a decade earlier, he was now the star of *The Graduate*, set in Pasadena. You truly never know how full circle success and failure will be.

Oh, and his friend and fellow actor who tied him for least likely to succeed? Gene Hackman, who spanned four decades of roles as one of the most prominent actors in the United States ever.

Least Likely to Succeed

We all feel at times that success is not for us. Whether someone has flat-out given us this award like Dustin Hoffman and Gene Hackman. Or someone has simply implied it or given us a name we cannot shake. We all feel at times that success is a fairy tale we once heard as kids.

Yet, the people who want to tell you that you're the least likely to succeed typically are speaking from a place of personal failure. They tried. They failed. So you will too.

Yes. You'll fail. We all do. But maybe failing is simply training in disguise. Like Dustin Hoffman selling hockey tickets as a pretend French Canadian.

Maybe failing is the best thing in the world that could be happening to you right now. Because it's forcing you to become better. Maybe failure is the path to your success, not a detour away from it.

What you deem as grand success now might not really stand for much later. And what you deemed as a failure now might become the launching pad for your greatest success later.

You don't need everyone to see your talent. Sometimes you just need one. It takes one yes to wipe away a hundred no's.

This too shall pass. Successes and failures both. You won't really know what worked and what didn't work until the very end. At that point, you might not really care.

NEXT STEPS:

- Maybe failing is simply training in disguise.
- Sometimes the only difference between failing and succeeding at something is perseverance. Like Hoffman and Hackman, they didn't let failure stop them. They simply treated it as a detour and continued moving toward their goal. Is there some pursuit in your life that you know you should not quit even though the world seems to be trying to stop you at every turn? Keep walking forward. Keep pushing. Like a trick wall, you might push on that one brick that opens the entire thing.
- Lots of people will imply that you should just quit because you're the least likely to succeed at whatever you're trying. But ask yourself, have they succeeded at what you're attempting? If the answer is no, how would they know if you can make it or not? Be wise about whom you're taking life advice from.

LIE #11

I need to stay constantly connected

> Every culture must negotiate with technology, whether it
> does so intelligently or not. A bargain is struck in which
> technology giveth and technology taketh away.
>
> —Neil Postman

We're escaping from reality while constantly creating our own digital one. Our kids playing in front of us while we watch videos on our phone of other people's kids playing. Our spouse sitting on the couch next to us while we look at pictures of someone else's spouse. Use to be, when you needed to get away, you took a stroll. Now, when you want to get away? You take a scroll.

We're scrolling through something. Reading through anything. Finding something about nothing. We act like we're starving, but from what? It's a compulsion. An addicting addiction. That pull to pull out our phone. To feed ourselves with our feed. The glut so you don't have to listen to your gut. We walk forward, eyes on the screen. We fully trust that cars won't hit us, as if our phone gives us Jedi powers. We run into poles, fall down stairs, walk in front of a speeding car, go headfirst into fountains while staring at our screens. Yet, amazingly, as we're falling, we're still able to hold our phones out of the water.

We feel we'll miss something if we don't check now, while we miss everything in our now. We know all about what's going on with our sophomore-year roommate's kids, a person we haven't spoken with in eleven years. Yet we miss what's going on with our own kids playing right in front of us.

Is it because our kids require something of us, while the images on the screen require nothing? Our spouse needs something from us. The image of the spouse doesn't.

We drive with one hand on the wheel and the other hand pressing our phone against it. We look back and forth from the road to the screen like we'll be able to react in time if a kid runs into the road, chasing his ball. We treat it like we're living in a video game where we can just hit the reset button if something goes terribly wrong.

What is real? Is our online world real? Is our physical world?

If a tree falls in the forest, yet no one is there to take a slo-mo video of it, did it actually happen?

We are investing most of our social time on acquaintances we don't want to see in person, while the people we do want to see in person, we don't have time for.

I go outside and look at the sunset for a minute. Then I mindlessly sit down and scroll through pictures for ten minutes, many of them pictures of the same sunset. I look up. It's dusk. The sunset is gone.

How many times do I go on the phone to do something, then after thirty minutes I put it down and realize I didn't do the one thing I went on the phone to do? So I jump back on the phone for another forty-five minutes before I realize I've forgotten to do the one thing again, but now I can't remember what that thing is.

I won't spend five minutes reading a book, but I will spend twenty-five minutes reading an elaborate internet thread of comments about the state of my local basketball team.

To escape having thoughts about what I really think. To constantly stay connected, no matter what ties in my life it's severing.

We have to examine this.

Amusing Ourselves to Death

Neil Postman wrote a book on how we will amuse ourselves to death through the entertainment of technology. He wrote this in 1985 because of the likes of *Sesame Street* and Walter Kronkite's news. When TV was a heavy box with a turn dial to snag six channels, maybe even seven or eight(!) if you curled the tinfoil just right around the stretched-out antenna ears.

Now, television is everywhere and in everything. The phone. The car. The gas station. The refrigerator. The watch. The wall. The bed. The tree. The toilet. Who knows where the possibilities need to end?

But now, TV is not really entertaining enough for us. We used to lament that we no longer had the attention span to read books. Now, honestly, we don't have the attention span to watch an entire twenty-two-minute sitcom on television. So we watch while having our phones out, one eye and ear on the show, the other eye mindlessly scrolling through a litany of nothing/everything. Then we ask the person sitting next to us what's going on in the show. **We're now distracting ourselves from our distractions.**

It's definitely easier to amuse ourselves to death now more than ever. Until next year, when it will be even easier. But that won't even compare to the year after that! Everyone streaming everything about anything that is nothing. Oh the joy!

And yet, our amusement now is not that amusing. When we're on the phone, it doesn't feel like we're amusing ourselves to death. It feels like we're distracting ourselves to death. We're headlining ourselves to death. We're updating ourselves to death. We're connecting ourselves to death. We're informing ourselves to death with information about all kinds of deaths—information that we can't, or don't, do anything with. It kind of feels deadly.

And everything now is smart, which kind of feels like it's making us more dumb. We don't have to figure out how to spell a word, read a clock, go outside and look at the sky—we ask whatever smart device is nearby to give us the answer. It's like we're constantly cheating on the test. But the teacher is the one giving us the answer key.

We check the phone not as much for entertainment as for escape. A numbing of sorts. A distraction from the distraction of all the distractions. And, most times, we don't choose to do it. We don't even want to do it. We are compelled to do it. Our fingers start scratching before we realize we have an itch. Like water, our bodies start to tell us it's been too long since our last drink. Like smoking another cigarette, we swear we will stop and get it under control. *But just after this next one.*

We can stop. But can we? Of course we can. But will we? We might, maybe. I'm sure that I'm not sure.

I talked before about Obsessive Comparison Disorder. I think we're also confronting a new addiction with its own unique traits—Obsessive Connection Disorder. The need to constantly be connected, which in turn leaves us incredibly disconnected.

As social scientist and clinical psychologist Sherry Turkle writes in *Reclaiming Conversations*, studies have shown that "we get a neurochemical high from connecting."[1] If I'm talking about this in severe disorder terms, it's because I think we're just at the forefront of seeing the severe disorders that emerge from this lifestyle that most of us have willfully, and knowingly unknowingly, adopted.

> The machine tends not only to create a new human environment, but also to modify man's very essence. He was made to eat when he was hungry and to sleep when he was sleepy; instead, he obeys a clock. He was made to have contact with living things, and he lives in a world of stone. He was created with a certain essential unity, and he is fragmented by all the forces of the modern world.
>
> — Jacques Ellul, *The Technological Society*, written in 1954

85

You don't have to look too far or too closely to see this played out right in front of our eyes. You look at a group of friends sitting at a table in a restaurant and they're all on their phones.

You go to a meeting at work that took a lot of coordinating to set up and is using a lot of resources (time, money, output) to make happen. And what's 85 percent of the room doing? Pretending they are looking at the notebook on their laps, which is partially covering their phone, as they scroll through social media. It's clearly obvious what they're doing, but no one really notices or says anything, because they're most likely doing it too.

I've spent a lot of time at playgrounds with my four kids over the last eight years, and I can't even tell you how *Lord of the Flies* that even a tiny playground can feel like. Parents are there, but they're not. They're present, while completely absent. What is it doing to our kids' minds and hearts to feel like they are alone, they are unseen, even when their parent is constantly right there with them? I don't say this as a guilt trip, I say this because I have been far too guilty of it myself.

Spending day after day with small kids can feel very lonely. The constantness of kids is continually wearing down every nerve until you feel like each one is a piece of raw flesh being chopped up by a sushi chef.

Yet, here's the problem: our escape into our phone does not decrease our loneliness—it heightens it. We are all escaping into a disconnecting connection.

Two of Apple's biggest investors, Jana and CalSTRS, which control about two billion dollars' worth of Apple shares as cited by CNBC, wrote a letter imploring "Apple to study the impact of excessive phone use on mental health." The letter also states: "It is also no secret that social media sites and applications for which the iPhone and iPad are a primary gateway are usually designed to be as addictive and time-consuming as possible, as many of their original creators have publicly acknowledged."[2]

According to a 2016 survey of children and their parents by Common Sense Media, "Half of teenagers in the United States feel like they are addicted to their mobile phones and report feeling pressure to immediately respond to phone messages."[3]

Yet, as Tony Fadell, co-inventor of the iPhone, tweeted out in response to a *Wall Street Journal* article about kids' addiction with smartphones, "Adults are addicts—not only kids!" Mr. Fadell then wrote: "Apple Watches, Google Phones, Facebook, Twitter—they've gotten so good at getting us to go for another click, another dopamine hit."[4]

Do we see the phone apart from our hand or do we see the phone as a part of our hand?

What happens when your connection device becomes more invasive? For example, something as seemingly simple as moving the constant connection device from your pocket or purse to your watch. Now you're wearing it on your skin. I have a friend who proudly boasted the amazingness of his smart watch, encouraging others to get the same.

Now he doesn't go more than two minutes without doing a quick flip of his wrist to check his watch. Even when playing an active game outside with him, he'll take repeated "smart watch breaks" right in the middle of the game. No amount of guilt trips, pleading, or scolds can break his trance. He's completely left us mentally and now his body is unfortunately just in the way.

I've seen him say, "Goodbye, I need to leave, I have something to do," then I'll start talking with someone else, and I swear ten minutes later, I glance up and he is still walking away from us on the path he started down ten minutes ago. He looks like a drunk person as he slowly weaves from left to right, absorbed in his smart watch, not really making any progress to his supposed destination, but seemingly not minding it or caring about whatever thing he needed to get to so un-quickly.

I used to get mad at this friend as he constantly checked his watch. I used to try and keep talking to him. Now, I don't even bother. I guess, in a sense, he and his watch have sufficiently trained me to do that. Because now I'll be in midsentence, he'll look at his watch, and I'll just stop talking. Really there's no point in continuing. I'll sit and wait, sometimes so long that I'll just pull out my phone, and we might not really talk again until one of us has to leave.

And this is only because of a watch with a tiny screen! But he's wearing it. It's touching his skin. It's a part of him. It took his inclination toward tech and turned it into an automatic Pavlovian response. I don't think he knows he's looking at the watch right in front me 75 percent of the time he's doing it.

Constant Disconnecting Connection

It goes back to Neil Postman's quote I mentioned at the beginning of this lie:

> Every culture must negotiate with technology, whether it does so intelligently or not. A bargain is struck in which technology giveth and technology taketh away.[5]

Our Internet of Everything giveth and it taketh away. If nothing else, we must wrestle with the answer to this equation. What is your tech giving you personally and what is it taking away?

We must become aware of all the ways we are unaware. Will we control it? I feel the pull of my phone every day like I'm in some 1970s sci-fi movie and this little box in my pocket is controlling me.

We need to be mindful of the ways that we're using technology mindlessly.

As Sherry Turkle aptly writes in *Reclaiming Conversations*, "We are forever elsewhere."[6]

I'd add that it feels like we're constantly escaping to anywhere else but here.

Why does our here and now need escaping? What are we escaping from?

Physical // Digital

We need some intentional Tech Free Zones in our lives, without even feeling the need to share pictures on Instagram or Twitter of how amazing we're doing without tech.

We spend time preparing a meal, then we don't even consciously taste one bite as we scroll through our phone and mindlessly shovel the food in.

We sit with a good friend and then pay more attention to our not-so-good friends on our phones. As Fred Rogers, star of the beloved TV show *Mister Rogers' Neighborhood*, poignantly explained in an interview with Charlie Rose: "The most important thing is that we're able to be one to one, you and I, with each other, at the moment. If we can be present, to the moment, with the person that we happen to be with at the moment. that's what's important."[7]

I don't believe our brains, hearts, and souls are created to purely live and have our beings in a digital world. I believe our senses are calling out to us to be used, to be uncaged and let go to explore. Our five senses all have something amazing to teach us, if we'll only let them. As Nancy Kanwisher of MIT's McGovern Institute for Brain Research explains, "Neurons seem to 'want' to receive input. When their usual input disappears, they start responding to the next best thing."[8]

When we lose the physical world, we lose ways that our brain was born to run. Synapses and neurons become lazy, like couch potatoes in our mind. I'm not saying do away with the digital world. It's not going anywhere. But as the digital reality becomes even

89

more pervasive into the physical reality, where it becomes harder and harder to distinguish the lines between the two, we need to be able to live and breathe in both worlds. We can't forsake the physical for purely the digital. Stepping outside and taking a walk in the park is firing up more neurons and synapses in our brain than the CEOs of the smartphones only wish they could come close to.

As well, numerous studies have presented evidence that going on a walk in nature reduces feelings of anxiety and depression, and improves mental health.[9]

A 2/5ths Life

The phone is so immersive, so controlling, yet it's only utilizing two of our senses. Most of the time just one. Our sense of sight, which sends the new glorious evergreen headline of "That Politician Will Be the Fiery End of the World for All of Us!" to our whole body. Sometimes our sense of hearing gets looped in. Yet, our senses of touch, taste, and smell are in the back room playing cards and wondering when they will be called up to the big show.

Now, I realize we're on the cusp of virtual reality, augmented reality, and artificial reality making everything not real feel more real. Yet, right now, if we're so compulsively immersed, just with our eyes looking at a small screen, what happens when the tech reaches three, four, or all five senses? What happens when the tech creates a whole new sixth sense that you can't experience without the tech? Will we be utterly powerless then?

None of this is going to stop here, right? The windshield of our car becoming a connected screen. The eyeglasses we wear. An entire room becoming a digital world we enter into.

What happens when we start embedding the devices within us so we can be fully plugged in? In our wrist, in our ear, our hand, who knows? Sounds like a low-budget sci-fi movie, but are we that far off?

> **If we are unable to be alone, we will be lonely.**
> —Sherry Turkle

What happens when artificial intelligence becomes so intelligent that we don't feel like we even need the fake online encounters with real people anymore? What happens when the machine becomes the easiest thing we speak to because it's programmed to meet our every need?

What happens when your computer knows you better than any person? When the algorithms and artificial intelligence take all of you and spit back only what it knows you want to hear? What then? What will *connection* be then? Especially with an awkward, real person you have to allow in and you in turn have to take time to discover.

Is our digital world the most real thing we experience in a day? Does our physical world feel like merely a distraction until we can get back to the virtual?

Is the (insert latest "smart" technology) a luxury or our necessity?

Industry, whatever it might sell, doesn't want you looking away from a screen. Because then it can't sell you anything. Industry doesn't want you hiking into the mountains to get away. Well, that is until that lease agreement gets finalized for their giant embedded mountain screen so that personal trainers can coach you up the mountain from within the mountain (if you have the special $6.99 app, that is—or else, you will just be shown commercials the entire hike, your payment for hiking this free mountain).

The Shallow // The Deep

Right now, I'm sitting with my laptop by a lake in 39-degree weather. My fingers feel the cold with each press of the keys. This is me trying to join two worlds—the tech that I am using as a tool to help me write this book, with nature, quiet, and prayer that gives my soul some substance.

Looking over this partially frozen lake and watching the ducks swim through. Feeling the breeze hit my cheek. Hearing the geese fly over my head and the wind of their descent into the water. It all gives me more clarity and inspiration than any TED Talk or productivity app. Because I can see it. I can smell it. I can feel it. I can hear it. And I can touch it.

I don't want to live a 2/5ths existence. I don't want to be fragmented in a constant disconnected connection. I want to live whole.

NEXT STEPS:

- What is the technology in your life giving you and what is it taking away? Write about it here.

- How can you be more intentional about the ways you are using technology in your life? This week, when you feel yourself pulling out your phone not for any specific reason but just to escape, try to catch yourself, then ask, "Why am I going on the phone right now? Do I need to?" At least this begins the process of us being more intentional and mindful about when and where we are jumping on our phone instead of acting mindlessly. Let's begin to create the habit of choosing to go on technology, rather than the habit of technology luring us into a trap.

- Choose nature more often. Choose prayer and silence more often. Choose to leave your phone on a shelf in your room more often.

- Let's control our technology instead of the other way around.

LIE #12

YOLO—You Only Live Once

Let's be honest here—twentysomethings shouting the latest life motto is typically synonymous with the world shuddering.

Whether it's yelling "YOLO" while jumping off a building to then shatter a leg or talking about having a FROYO FOMO, these kinds of life mantras can cement every negative generational stereotype in stone.

YOLO. You only live once. Really? If you live to be 90 years old, you're not going to live once. You're going to live 32,850 days. That's 788,400 hours of life!

Honestly, if we wanted a more accurate slogan to replace YOLO, it would be YODO. You only die once. So instead of yelling YOLO while you jump off a building, maybe you should think YODO and just slowly climb your way back down and drink a nice cup of tea.

While we're at it, instead of whatever motto is all the rage right now, maybe some of these below would be better to live by in your twenties.

15 New Twentysomething Mottos to Live By

1. HYBO—Hustle Your Butt Off
2. WFH—War for Hope
3. POGO—Push On, Grit On

4. GO—Grit On
   You can't have a good story without a good struggle. Grit On, my friends.

5. KOB—Keep On Believing

6. CUSH—Create Until Something Happens
   We need more people passionate about creating solutions. Don't stop CUSHing it.

7. The MHU—The Many. The Humbled. The Unemployed.
   There are a lot of us! Be proud. Be brave. Keep WFH (warring for hope).

8. BHBC—Be Humble, Be Confident
   Have a quiet, humble confidence that shows up every day and does great work. Even when it feels like no one cares or notices, POGO.

9. CSED—Compliment Someone Every Day
   The most powerful networking tool you possess is well-timed, well-thought, intentional compliments. A meaningful compliment will open up more doors than any résumé will.

10. LLUMI—Live Like You Mean It

11. MUNIC—My, You Need Insightful Counsel
    Okay, kind of a reach here. But we all need advice, and more importantly, wise counsel.

12. HOPE—Hold On, Purpose Evolves
    As you war for hope, remember HOPE—hold on, purpose evolves. Even if it doesn't feel like life is turning out like it was "supposed to," the bigger you feel your purpose is, the more preparation it will take to get there.

13. DYA—Define Your Anxiety
    I've learned that when I'm feeling anxious, I need to stop, think, and define where my anxiety is coming from.
    Once you've defined what your anxiety actually is you can do something about it.

14. STAT—Set the Adult Table

    You've moved from the kids' table to the adult table. No more plastic sporks and tiny chairs for you.

    Start setting the adult table so you're ready when the sweet food starts coming your way from your successful HYBO.

15. WIDEL—When In Doubt, Enjoy Life

    This is not another definition of YOLO; this is a call to appreciate, enjoy, and savor each season you're in—the good, the bad, and the awkward. There is amazing going on all around you if you're willing to look for it.

NEXT STEPS:

- Take one of these slogans that really resonates with you and tape it to your mirror. Work on making that a habit you focus on creating that week. For example, CUSH—Create Until Something Happens. Got a problem you're facing? Work on creating a solution. Push past where you think you can go, and go further.

- If none of these slogan resonate with you, write your own. What makes you tick and gets you excited? What's a habit you can begin working on this week?

- Feel like slogans are ridiculous? Great, run with that. I think we'd all be living healthier lives if we consistently chose age-old wisdom over the new catchy slogan that we won't believe we said ten years from now.

LIE #13

I'm such a failure

Have you seen the incredible documentary about folk musician Sixto Rodriguez called *Searching for Sugar Man*? If you haven't, please go watch it now because I'm going to spoil the ending here. As we analyze this lie, I want to highlight two men from the documentary—one who lived by an incredible truth, and one who started living a terrible lie.

If you haven't watched it and want to cut to the chase with me, Sixto Rodriguez was a '70s folk musician from the streets of Detroit who was in the same vein as Bob Dylan. When Sixto was starting out playing in dark and smoky bars, he still felt too "seen" and would perform with his back to the audience.

Sixto catches his big break, records an album, and it goes nowhere. He records some more songs to the same unacclaim and then it's over for him. His music career stalls out, and he goes back to Detroit, working in the demolition industry. He works decades of hard manual labor, but with the same love and purpose that he did for his music as he helps rescue old buildings and breathe new life into them. Then as well, he never stopped playing music. It still was a part of him, even if the world seemingly didn't care to hear it.

But as the documentary, and Swedish director Malik Bendjelloul, so aptly shows, while Rodriquez thinks his music sunk to the bottom of the sea, the ripples had been growing into a revolution on the other side of the world! A bootlegged copy of his music had made its way to South Africa years ago, and his lyrics were a national protest cry for a culture trying to break out of apartheid and censorship. Rodriquez thought his music was a failure. Instead, his music was inspiring a generation. He thought he'd die an unknown. In South Africa he was a legend.

Many in South Africa heard rumors that Sixto Rodriguez had died years ago. They didn't know he was demoing homes in Detroit. Then finally record store owner Bob Sugarman in South Africa tracked down Sixto, and to Rodriguez's utter amazement, twenty-eight years after his music record *Cold Facts* was released, he would be flown out to South Africa to play six huge concerts where fans wouldn't stop cheering for five minutes when he first walked onstage. The Beatles and the Rolling Stones were nice little bands in South Africa compared to the superstar that was Sixto Rodriquez.

You never know where your dream will take you. You never know how much further your dream will go than you ever could've imagined.

While the Liar would try to have Rodriquez give it all up, and possibly end his life like all the rumors suggested, Sixto kept doing what he was made to do. Purposeful work while playing music. The outcome wasn't originally what he hoped for, but he wasn't going to let that stop him from living from a place of meaning and truth.

Then years later, he'd be rewarded in finding a huge following for his music in South Africa and Australia, and then through the documentary, which won an Oscar in 2013. Sixto Rodriquez's faithfulness to the truth would be rewarded in a powerful, visible, and—in his own words—"fairy-tale" kind of way.

And yet, there was a dark side that emerged from *Searching for Sugar Man*. Good-looking, talented, extremely smart, visionary director Malik Bendjelloul. He'd spent years following the story of Sixto Rodriquez, and then 1,000 hours editing the documentary, overcoming many obstacles on the way as investors pulled out after seeing his first cut because they thought it was terrible. But in an incredible story of perseverance about this incredible story of perseverance, *Searching for Sugar Man* would win an Oscar for Best Documentary in 2013. Bendjelloul quickly became one of the most talked-about directors in the world.

Then just a year later, he would step in front of a speeding subway car in Sweden and tragically end his own life. If that transition feels stark, it's because it was.

When I heard the news, I was completely shocked. From watching interviews with his family and friends, they were even more so. While making sense of suicide can be a hard and impossibly painful endeavor, his friends had various perspectives on what led to this tragic event. To some, it seemed like the pressure following his Oscar-winning documentary was becoming too much for Bendjelloul. He wasn't sleeping. He was losing contact with friends. He was turning down small assignments because they felt too overwhelming. And in the end, it quickly became all too much.[1]

Bendjelloul had poured every ounce of energy and artistic flair he had into *Sugar Man*, and now that it was over, he was struggling to find a new passion, said his friends. In the final weeks, he told those closest to him, a fear had taken hold that somehow, inexplicably, he had "lost his creativity."

The juxtaposition of Rodriquez and Bendjelloul breaks my heart and unnerves me.

Here I am feeling overwhelmed as I stare at blank pages. Here I am fearing that I have nothing more to offer, when just this year I had a somewhat *Sugar Man* experience myself.

A bootlegged copy of my third book *101 Questions You Need to Ask in Your Twenties* was translated into Farsi and released in Iran. To my wildest amazement, these last six months I've probably had more Iranians reaching out to me through social media to tell me how much my book has impacted them than I've had from twentysomethings in the United States. Unbelievable.

If I would have set out to strategically write a book to speak to Iranians, there's no way I could've pulled it off. And yet, in the same fairy-tale kind of way, it happened. I even had one Iranian reader reach out to say they were thinking of ending their own life before reading my book and now they had hope. An amazing, and humbling, thing for me to read.

You see, we really can't live for the outcome.

We can't judge our worth on the outcome.

We can't even judge our successes or failures by the outcomes. We are wildly inaccurate when we claim something as a complete failure. How can we possibly know?

The immediate outcome is one minute of our lives. Who knows what will happen in the thousands of minutes that follow? What we see as a failure now could be the exact stepping-stone we need years from now. What we see as a failure now could lead to our greatest success later.

Like Vincent van Gogh, who would sell only one painting in his lifetime and was by all accounts a failed artist, to only start to receive recognition for his paintings twenty years after his death.

Sixto Rodriquez is a wild success story that took thirty years to grow and blossom. What his record company deemed a failure was igniting hope and speaking truth to an entire country fighting through apartheid.

Malik Bendjelloul worked on his documentary for years with investors pulling out midway through because they thought what he had so far was complete rubbish. He had to finish graphics and editing all on his own. He had persevered through so much and then saw the wildest fruition of his dreams come true when he won the Oscar for Best Documentary. Yet, the better-than-he-could've-ever-imagined outcome didn't make him feel like a success. Unfortunately, the tragic opposite happened.

Positive or negative outcomes are not the cause of unhappiness. There are plenty of very unhappy people who have gotten everything their heart desired. Whether the outcome was exactly what we wanted or whether the outcome was the exact opposite, we can be just as disillusioned or disappointed. The outcome is probably the worst thing to judge your success or failure on.

Making Progress?

Even the progress to our outcome might not look like we wanted it to.

If you're measuring your success solely by the progress you can see, you'll be beating your dream to a pulp with a measuring stick that you and your dream will never measure up to.

Progress is rarely what we think it is. We measure progress by what we can see, when progress is really the roots that are slowly, yet purposefully, expanding underground.

People who walked by the small saplings at the park years ago come back and can't believe the giant oak trees they are now.

You live with your kids every day, and yet it's only when you see a picture from years ago that you realize how much they've grown right in front of your eyes.

Seeing progress is not about just what you can see. Seeing progress is letting yourself *believe in all that is unseen.*

Making "progress" might mean you're one failure closer to a success.

Basically, do good work. Don't sacrifice your character along the way. Learn. Grow. And the outcome sitting in front of you, good or bad, will have nothing to do with your success or failure.

As we see in the story of Sixto Rodriguez and director Malik Bendjelloul, an amazing outcome can break you and a terrible outcome can lead to long-term success. We think the outcome is the entire point, when it is just another small step on the journey. If we make the whole journey about the predetermined outcome we envisioned, we are destined to be disappointed and disillusioned, no matter if the outcome was good or bad.

Or as Maya Angelou said: "Success is liking yourself, liking what you do, and liking how you do it."[2]

All Groan Up

For me personally, I poured more years of my life and more of my soul into my second published book, *All Groan Up: Searching for Self, Faith, and a Freaking Job!* And after eight years of failing, hoping, believing, editing, rewriting, being rejected by one publisher three different times, that same publisher would end up publishing it years later. When people read the book, they wrote me some of the deepest, most personal messages in return. It seemed like the book was really speaking to people from a heart level. Problem was, not many people read it! It was a publishing failure.

Honestly, the failed outcome really hurt. I didn't see all the successes and progress I'd made. I just saw the low sales numbers.

To work for so long, put so much of yourself into something, and finally see it happen, and then have it only make the sound of uneaten leftovers being dropped into the trash can. That was hard. Once it was pretty clear that the book wasn't going to "make it," I grieved. I really did. I had to let the book go almost like I was attending its funeral. Might sound melodramatic, but if you've had a dream die, you can probably understand the pain.

> **It's not about what you're doing, it's about who you're becoming. Inside yourself and amongst yourself.**
> —Frederick Buechner

In 2019, four years after *All Groan Up* released, I received an email through the State of Tennessee Penitentiary System. It appeared I had a message from a prisoner there. I thought it was a joke or spam. I wasn't sure if I should accept the message or not, but for whatever reason, it felt like the real deal. So I accepted it. I was nearly brought to tears by what I read, and we started a back-and-forth correspondence.

The prisoner told me her story. How long she'd been in prison and what for. She told me she had been struggling, but then in prison she found and read my book *All Groan Up*. It had given her hope. She started believing she had a future. I was shocked and humbled. A reminder to me that I'm just playing one instrument and God is conducting the whole orchestra.

I was so encouraged by this dialogue, about the hope that sprung out of my failure, that I grieved. But then I realized something. It was probably *only* because the book was a failure in sales, not in spite of it, that *All Groan Up* found its way to the Tennessee State Penitentiary. It was probably a donation to the prison from the publisher because they still had so many copies left over! If *All Groan Up* was a success by sales number standards, it probably would have never made it to that prison cell to bring hope to that person. The failure of the book was its pathway into one of the hardest places in the world to enter.

What you see as a failure now might save someone's life later.

You never know who you are encouraging and breathing life into, no matter how it feels or looks to you right now. Your kids who you don't think are listening. Your friend who feels distant. Your coworker who feels like they're slipping away. You might never know the impact you're really having, but that doesn't mean it's not happening.

As I first asked in *101 Questions You Need to Ask in Your Twenties*, "Who will you not be able to help if you give up now?"

While we will never fully know the answer to this question from where we sit right now, I think this is an important question to

> **A man who fails well is greater than one who succeeds badly.**
>
> —Thomas Merton

keep at the core of any dream. Because someone is going to need you and your dream. Someone is going to need your resolution as you slogged through failed outcomes. Someone is going to need your perseverance. Because as they lose hope, you will provide a lifeline from having been there and done that.

It's that question of "who will I not be able to help if I give up now?" that's kept me going through many rejection letters and failed outcomes. Because that question ties into my deeper motivations. It goes past financial gains and losses. It transcends further than the amount of likes I get or don't get.

The pain and struggle you've personally had to go through in life become a secret sauce of sorts for persevering through immediate failure. When you're working toward solving a problem that has been personally frustrating or painful to you, then each failure along the way won't have the same kind of power to stop you. You know what it's like to have to go through this, and you're going to be more willing to push through failure and obstacles when trying to help others get through the same thing. Persevering becomes deeply personal because of the pain you've experienced, not in spite of it. **What we see as our pain now might be our purpose later.**

Then, the next failure that comes along doesn't become your death sentence. No, it will just be a regular old sentence that you simply erase and rewrite.

Persevering Principles

Persevering through failure becomes more possible when you're pursuing something that fits your skill set and strengths, so you enjoy the day-to-day process of doing it. Then as well, you're pursuing a goal that ties into something deeply important to you, maybe because you've experienced personal pain and frustration from it yourself. And you know how important it is for you to keep going so you can be there for others who are going through the same thing.

We can't cling too tightly to what we perceive are the outcomes in the present. **Outcomes can only be seen through the lens of eternity.** And since we don't exactly have that kind of sight, I think we're all better off if we don't stare at our immediate outcomes for too long.

A year from now, three years, five years, ten years, twenty-eight years (like Sixto Rodriquez), someone, possibly someone from across the world, might need your breath of life. Your "failures" might be sparking a revolution of hope and you might not know a thing about it. Someone might be hanging off a cliff with three fingers still barely clinging to the edge, and you and your dream will be there to lift them up and help save their life. So as you go through your twenties and thirties, with a myriad of supposed failures and successes, don't make the outcomes more than they are—whether good or bad. It's one small stone on the path. You can either pick up that stone and throw it through your car window for all of social media to see, or you can simply take a step on it and keep walking forward. It's your choice.

NEXT STEPS:

- What we deem as a success or failure now might become the exact opposite later. Let's stop looking at failures as a death sentence instead of just a sentence to rewrite before we create our next one.

- Perseverance becomes more possible when we're doing something we enjoy and is personally important to us to see it through. Write down some skills and strengths you really enjoy utilizing on a day-to-day basis. Then write down some painful or frustrating things you've gone through that you would love to help others get through.

LIE #14

My life doesn't look like it was "supposed to"

"Supposed to" is a lie. Life will never look or feel like it's "supposed to." Especially in your twenties.

I wrote about this first in *101 Secrets for Your Twenties*, and I'm more sure of this truth now than ever. Because what is "supposed to"? "Supposed to" is built on some sort of expectation or pressure that is bound to disappoint you. Because it's not real. Nowadays our "supposed to" is built on everyone's curated success on social media. We "see" what "success" looks like online through snapshots of friends and, sometimes even worse, influencers. Yet the snapshot they are showing us of what success is "supposed to" look like couldn't be further from the truth.

Life in our twenties, life in general, is messy most times. Often you might feel like you're living in completely paradoxical worlds of success and failure, glamour and the grind, all at the exact same time. And none of it feels or looks like what you thought it would. It's living out the paradox of the process.

Going through a Hailstorm in a Convertible

In our midtwenties, my wife and I felt like we were supposed to go to a financial conference in Austin, Texas, to learn some financial wisdom. Problem was, we didn't have much money. So first, instead of flying to Austin from Los Angeles, we hopped into my wife's Mazda Miata soft-top convertible and drove straight through for twenty hours to get there. If you've ever ridden in a Mazda Miata, you know it's not exactly the largest car in the world. It fit my wife perfectly. For me, a road trip in the Miata was like getting hugged by all sides of the car for twenty hours straight.

Then since there's a big conference in town, of course that means all the hotels within twenty miles start charging you like they are taking you on a Royal Caribbean cruise. So here come the Angones rolling in at 10:00 p.m., in Austin, and going to our hostel.

As we get the grand tour of the hostel from one of the group leaders, we start realizing this is less of a hostel and more of a commune that people live at full-time. They just had one open room, as the previous occupant had either moved out in the middle of the night, or died (we couldn't get it confirmed one way or the other). But as we stepped into our "room," we had become pretty sure that death was the cause of the previous tenant's removal, as it was a slab of cement with some interesting stains on the walls. The only thing in the room was a mattress on the floor.

If this room sounds a little scary, it was! But hey, I considered this a big step up from sleeping in the Mazda Miata!

I'll never forget sleeping on this concrete slab in this commune, getting up early in the morning, meticulously putting on our best business suits, and then going to a financial conference to learn from and network with the rich and successful. The ludicrousness of our current reality mixed with the reality we were trying to move into was not lost on us. This was not how it was "supposed to" look for attendees of this conference, but it was how it looked for us. It was what it was and we really didn't care. We learned a lot at the conference. And we didn't die at the commune. It was a win-win.

Driving back home to Los Angeles, in the middle of the wide-open plains of Texas, huge, dark clouds quickly rolled in. The closer we got to the clouds, the more terrifying they looked. As we neared a bridge overpass that provided some shelter, every inch of cover was taken by big trucks and trailers looking to hide out from the storm. There was no room for us. There was no turning around. There was no place to hide. So what did we do in our toy car Miata with a soft top? We put our foot on the gas, honked at the hiding trucks, and drove right on past them all and into the heart of the storm.

Five minutes later, I thought every inch of the convertible top was going to be ripped in pieces from pounding hail. But we drove through the heart of the storm and came out the other side. A few dents for the experience, but we were still driving. And yeah, again, we were still alive.

Fitting metaphor for our twenties. Big storms come in fast. You're scared. You're unprepared. And your only chance of survival is to step on the gas and drive on through.

It was slightly dangerous. A little reckless. A lot of adventure. And a big memory that will stick with us for the rest of our marriage.

None of it looked like it was supposed to and that's exactly how it was supposed to be. Had we taken an airplane there and stayed in a comfy hotel, we'd have removed three-fourths of our memories of the entire trip and put a hefty bill on our credit card.

If you're pursuing what success is "supposed to" look like in your life, I'm not sure what kind of success you're going to find. If you want the path toward pursuing something bigger to look pretty and put-together, well, friend, that ain't happening.

Our twenties are a giant contradiction of sorts. It's feeling like a success and a failure all in the same moment, sometimes at the same lunch. It's lots of moments of sacrificing comfort for calling. Of putting in lots of work and not having a ton of "real" things to brag about on social media.

It's working hard for months and giving an amazing sales presentation at work, then driving back in your used Toyota to your studio apartment and eating a bowl of Cap'n Crunch.

Embrace the messiness of it. Be comfortable in the awkwardness of it all. Don't worry if you're 100 percent not looking or feeling the part.

Don't worry that it doesn't resemble what you thought it was supposed to. Because I'm coming to understand from my own life and from meeting with others around me that your thirties, forties, fifties, sixties, retirement, marriage, having kids—none of it will feel or look like it's supposed to. Life is full of surprises all along the way. We no longer have to be surprised by that.

"Supposed to" is a lie. You're free from its hold.

Live like you need to, not like you're supposed to.

NEXT STEPS:

- Can you spot any "supposed to's," some expectations that haven't exactly gone as you planned, that are holding you back and keeping you from moving into what is in front of you? You keep thinking about what was "supposed to" happen instead of what is going on. Maybe it's even someone you have a lot of bitterness and blame toward (a parent, friend, teacher, God) because you feel they didn't come through for you like they were "supposed to." Write it down. It's hard to move past something that is nameless. Name it. Wrestle with it. Grieve it, if need be. Then, it's easier to lay it down and begin to walk forward in a new, fresh way. What you thought was "supposed to" happen, didn't happen. So let yourself start seeing the reality in front of you, and do something about it.

LIE #15

Nostalgia

In the movie *500 Days of Summer*, Tom is trying to get Summer back. They dated. They fell in love. They broke up. Tom is desperate to win her back. Throughout the movie, Tom thinks back to all the wonderful memories they shared. At the café. At the record store. Watching a movie together. All the fond memories. Tom is heartbroken.

Yet, it's Tom's preteen sister who sits him down to try and talk some sense into him.

"Look, I know you think she was the one, but I don't. Now, I think you're just remembering the good stuff. Next time you look back, I really think you should look again."[1]

Then we see the same nostalgic scenes that Tom has been replaying over and over, yet this time we see the memory in its entirety. We see Summer pull her hand back when Tom reaches out. We see Summer bawling in the movie theater. Not because she's touched by the movie. But because they're watching the end of *The Graduate* and the final scene of Dustin Hoffman ("Benjamin") and Katharine Ross ("Elaine") in the back of the bus, together, with no idea where they're headed in a relationship that is most likely going to end in disaster because Ben has already had an affair with Elaine's mom. Not exactly a great first ingredient in the recipe for long-term relationship success.

Summer is bawling not because she's in love with Tom, but she most likely is seeing their relationship on the same ill-fated bus ride.

When Tom "looks again," he starts seeing the truth. That maybe his nostalgic memories of the relationship he swore was The One was kind of doomed for failure since their first kiss in the copy room. Throughout the movie you feel for Tom and you blame Summer, but as actor Joseph Gordon Levitt, who played Tom, even recently said in an interview: "Tom's biases, Tom's lack of being able to see what's real . . . I think it's Tom's fault. Tom's not listening to Summer."[2]

At one point or another, nostalgia lies to all of us. Whether it's like Tom as we think back on a relationship, obsessing over the five great memories and forgetting about the fifty terrible ones. Or it's thinking back to those "best days of our life" that we couldn't wait to escape when we were in them. But now that we're out and confused, we want to go back.

Nostalgia is the lie of wanting something back that never actually was.

Because it was never that good. It wasn't perfect. The past had its problems too.

There are no best years of your life. Every season has the good, the bad, the awkward, the beautiful, and the ugly.

Enjoy the good. Forget about the bad. Then leave both in the past where they belong.

Nostalgia is just an idyllic story we tell ourselves of the past when we are afraid of the future. Or we're finding it difficult to be present in our present. But how will you ever step into that future if you're always looking backward?

It's hard to live today if you're obsessing about how things were better yesterday. Whether it be a past relationship, school, friendship, or season of life. If you're always trying to get back to the way things used to be, you will never go anywhere new.

Nostalgia is like drinking a big cup of eggnog when you're lactose intolerant. It might taste sweet and comforting going down, but it sure is going to make you hunker down on the toilet later.

I love good memories of times past. Sometimes it is important to remind ourselves of what we've made it through and the many blessings we've been given in life. This gives us a good perspective to tackle our current problems. But I know the moment I start obsessing over those memories is the moment I start getting really sad. When I put on that old album that we listened to through our senior year of college, I start thinking about what *was* instead of focusing on what *is* and what's yet to come.

The future has some amazing new memories in store for you, if you'll let it. The present has so much to offer. It is ripe with new memories waiting to be discovered. But we have to have our eyes open to them. We can't let the lies of nostalgia blind us to the "amazing new" all around us. More success, more amazing memories await you in the future. But we won't be able to see it if we're obsessed with trying to reinvent the past.

Nostalgia is living in a dream of the past instead of being alive and awake in the present.

Tom, in the movie *500 Days of Summer*, finally in his heart let Summer go. He moved on from the past. He interviewed for a new job. His eyes were reopened to new relationships and new possibilities. So in the interview room, he knows something meaningful has just happened when he strikes up a conversation with a new woman, Autumn.

You have to be willing to live in the "unknown now." The past is in the past. The future is in the future. The now is now. It's the only place where new memories can be made. It's the only place that you are currently alive.

Don't deny the fruit of the present and the future by constantly choking on the dry crusts of the past.

NEXT STEPS:

- Do you have any best times of your life that you find yourself wishing you could go back to or thinking about too often? Write them down.

- Now, look at the life you're experiencing right now, but look at it like you're five years in the future. What will you miss about today? What are you possibly taking for granted? For me, I think about my kids. As a dad of four young ones, I will say they sometimes can find that last thread of parental patience I have as they get into a drop-dead fight over a green marble, and my last thread is ripped in pieces. But I know five years from now I'll greatly miss this season of them being this age. I'll miss all the beautiful moments of each day. I'll miss the toddles, shrieks, songs, and smiles. So instead of being nostalgic about them in the future, why not just be intentional about enjoying them now at 7:00 a.m. on a Monday? We don't have to wait for nostalgia to appreciate our life. We can just appreciate it now.

LIE #16

But I worked so hard

This might be the greatest inside joke of the twenty-first century that we all kind of know is not true but are hoping no one blows our cover. Are we consistently lying to ourselves about how hard we worked? Most times, I think we are.

As a salaried employee for years, I can definitely relate to this. When you're working a sales job, if you don't produce, they're going to let you go. When you're working a salary job, you're first and foremost judged on your ability to sit in a chair by 8:00 a.m. and not leave that chair until 5:00 p.m.

Your butt, in a chair, at the proper time. It's like the adult version of musical chairs. Except there's no music. And you don't move. But there's office birthday cake! Or donuts. Or a big glass bowl of chocolates in the lobby that are supposed to be for clients that you secretly watch and wait for the receptionist to leave their chair so you can make a covert dash to the front for a handful that you shove in your pocket when the receptionist comes around the corner and then you have to quickly search for something to say like you had a reason other than stealing chocolates and all you can think of is, "So how's your cat doing? Is she good?"

In every office there's always the employee who never comes late and never leaves early, so the boss consistently applauds them in meetings for the example they set. Except for the fact that they haven't, you know, really done their actual job for about five years now. You know it. They know it. The boss kind of knows it but is just glad that at least one person is following the rules. So they give them a plaque and $10 bonus bucks to use at the employee gift shop.

Salaried jobs are where hard work goes to take a nap.

Oh, you're going to make me sit in this seat for how many hours of my week? Oh, I will for sure reward you with boundless, bustling productivity as years are removed from my lifespan for my complete lack of human movement.

Even if you want to work hard, you can't. I think many of us start the job gung-ho, tackling projects, asking for more responsibilities, asking questions about systems in place and how we can do things better. But then you become *that* coworker. You are trying to blow the cover off the whole office, and your coworkers' stares and whispers in the halls will let you know that the next time you go to the break room, they are going to come in behind you, close the door, and have a "come to Jesus" intervention with you.

Then you start learning a solid truth—a salaried employee is a person who has gotten very creative at taking two hours of actual work and spreading it across the entire day.

Case in point: when you're out sick a few days. Like actually sick. Not you got a great deal on a plane ticket to Maui and you're going to make the ultimate sacrifice of not posting any pictures of the trip online so that you can "be sick" and go. No, you got the flu like you just licked the monkey bars at the playground.

So after a few days off without touching an ounce of work, you show up and you cringe at the thought of what your inbox looks like. But you're full of cold medicine and caffeine, and you're fired up to catch up. You start hammering away. You're working. You're feeling alive. An energy and flow surging through you like you haven't experienced for years. You're like a blacksmith at the fire pounding on the metal until you answer that last email, put some finishing touches on that project, and then, you're done. You're all caught up. You lean back in your chair, proud of your accomplishments. Then you look at the clock: *11:30 a.m.?!* You just did two and a half days of real work in three and a half hours. Wow, that's something.

Entrepreneurs Too

It's not just salaried employees though.

Being an entrepreneur can present the exact opposite problem. No one is telling you when you have to come into work and when you have to leave. So . . . you start "work" at 10:00 a.m., which basically means you watch fifteen minutes of Jim Gaffigan on YouTube, check your emails, scroll through Instagram, throw up a tweet that took you five tries and twenty-five minutes to come up with, and then you head to lunch at 12:00. You had every intent of working after lunch, but you got a little sleepy after the heavy meal. And the fourth round of Wimbeldon is on ESPN3, which of course you now need to become fully engrossed in for the next week.

How many times has an hour of work on the computer meant five minutes of actual work mixed in with fifty-five minutes of social-media *internetness.*

Or I laughably think of some of my days as a college student. Sure, there were some semesters where I was going nonstop, like my first year of college when I was playing football and baseball while holding a full schedule of classes. I'd be up at 5:30 a.m. for morning weight training and conditioning, walking across a dark campus in Nebraska in December, when the bitter, cold wind was cutting me to pieces like a mean midwestern ninja. Then it would be a full day of classes and studying. Then baseball practice would start at 10:00 p.m. in the gym and go to midnight. And this was during the off season of both sports.

But then there were the slack-off semesters of my college career. You know, the ones when you went to class in the morning, then lunch for two hours with seven friends. Then you barely made it to your second, and last, class of the day. Then volleyball. Dinner. Study for fifteen minutes. Watch a TV show. And you thought you were working hard!

There were also semesters where you had classes with wise professors who were teaching you all these amazing things and the room was full of ripe discussion and you were surrounded by friends, and yet, you missed five classes and almost failed because the class was at 8:00 a.m.! And gosh, that's just a little too much to ask.

Then you step into the working world after college and realize that a day filled with learning and discussion with a wise professor would be like the most amazing day of your entire year, and you're taking vacation days just to go and try to sit in on some classes again!

Land of Make-Believe

Whatever season of life, or wherever we find ourselves working, I find that we far too easily trick ourselves into thinking we are actually working hard. And please know, I'm writing this for myself more than anyone else. As I attempt to write, I constantly find myself wasting time trying to find the proper way, time, and place to use my time wisely. I can quickly become a walking paradox of inefficiency.

Yet, time in and of itself is not a pure indicator of hard work. That's often the first lie we tell ourselves. "But I worked so long on this!" The amount of time you spend with something doesn't mean the production or quality of work is inherently there.

Or God bless you if your work requires you to do research on the internet. Good luck with that. Researching on the internet is like walking into a busy New York City subway because you want your alone time.

117

It's not that researching on the internet is bad for the amazing things we're quickly able to find. It's problematic for all the things on the internet that find you.

But you took up four hours doing it! And you were on your computer the whole time! Surely that should count for something! Now, I know there are people on opposite sides of this coin. Those who work all the time. Those who can't stop working. Those who go on a vacation because they're forced to and then find themselves yelling at the Polynesian dancers to keep it down at the luau because they're on an important webinar about the integrative marketing strategy of using the CMS effectively for full B2B ROI and higher CTR by the EOD.

Yeah, I don't fully understand these people either. There have been times in my life when I've found myself working too much, but they've been a few fleeting specks in the middle of a blizzard of complacency.

What Does It Mean to Work Hard? How Do We Do It?

It helps to work hard if you feel like the work you're doing actually means something to you.

It helps if you understand why you're doing the work and for what end.

It helps if you understand the role you and your work play in the greater scheme of things.

It helps if you know that if you don't do the work, no one will do it for you, which coincides with the fact that no one is going to pay your bills either, so you better do some dang work.

It helps if you're not waiting to feel inspired so that you can then be productive. Working, oftentimes, is like being dropped into the middle of a lake. You didn't feel like swimming beforehand, but by golly, you better start moving those arms and legs if you're going to stay afloat. As I first wrote in *101 Questions You Need to Ask in Your Twenties*, "Sometimes the most inspired thing you can do is keep showing up when you're completely uninspired."[1] Show up. Start working. Let the inspiration follow instead of trying to constantly find and follow inspiration.

It helps to also incorporate learning and trying new things as a part of your work. Work doesn't always mean productivity on paper. It could be productively working on learning a new skill or technique. It could be productively reading a book that's making you think deeper and become a better human being. That's work that pays off too.

It also helps to be intentional about your breaks from work. Instead of jumping on social media, maybe a break from work is taking a walk outside if you can. Or meeting with a coworker or friend for coffee to build a better relationship.

It helps if you know what times of the day work best for you to do certain kinds of work. Let me explain.

I know if I need to write or creatively dive into a big project, I need to do that first thing in the morning. Not look at emails. Not do social media. Not schedule any meetings or phone calls. I have my best energy and ability in that 9:00 a.m. to noon slot, and I need to protect that time like a mama lion protecting her cub from all the time-sucking hyenas out there.

If I don't get the hard work done that I need to, then the good Lord knows it ain't happening at 2:00 p.m. when that caffeine crash is shoving my head toward my desk like a fifth-grade bully.

It All Adds Up

Your hard work or your lack of hard work all adds up. It builds off itself. And sometimes the real work you need to do is pretty unglamorous before you can get to the work you really want to do.

Success in your twenties and thirties is like painting a house. It takes a lot of scraping, sanding, scrubbing, prepping, and priming before you can even paint one brushstroke. And if you decide to skip the REAL WORK before the work, then your paint will all just crack and flake away.

I learned this metaphor all too well this past summer when my wife and I made a deal—she would fly, by herself, with all four kids to California (my wife is brave!) to vacation with her family. While I would stay home and work on the peeling, cracking, outdated front of our house and attempt to update it with some curb appeal and love.

It was a process. Replacing siding, prepping my house (with the fifteen steps described above), painting my house (with multiple coats), making cedar window boxes and shutters, and putting them up in 95-degree heat. It was brutally exhausting. Yet, when I could stand back and look at the transformation of my house, it was deeply gratifying. Then when my family got home from vacation and I was able to do a "Fixer Upper" reveal for my wife, the delight and surprise on her face made every minute of work more than worth it. The work was hard, it made a difference, and it was incredibly rewarding.

Reworking Work

Here's where I get my most overwhelming and abundant feelings of contentment, purpose, and well-being:

Intentional times with my family

Intentional times of building meaningful relationships with others

Intentional times of quiet and prayer

Intentional times of working and creating

You see, work is one-quarter of my contentment pie. And in my opinion, I think that's a good percentage to keep it in. I think some people make work the whole pie and then divorce, discontentment, and despair ensue when they realize they alienated everything else in their life. And then they get fired and are really in for a crash.

Yet, on the flip side, another lie of culture is when work is not part of our equation for a meaningful life and emotional wellbeing. Instead, we view work as something we have to do, something that should be endured for fifty years so that we can retire and never have to work again. Then we retire and become depressed because we have nothing to do!

Instead, I think work should be a constant source of life, meaning, and purpose as we serve others with the work of our hands by doing good work in a way that only we can do.

Work is a joy. I really mean that. I am way happier after working hard and getting to appreciate the work I've been able to accomplish than when I go do something that is supposed to "make me happy," like watching a movie or wasting time online. Most of the things that we do with the sole purpose of making us happy oftentimes feel empty, while working at something meaningful, and completing it, fills our world with a depth of contentment like no other.

Yes, there will always be parts of our job we will not fully enjoy. And there will be seasons of life where work really feels like a laborious duty that is bringing little joy.

But I guess I don't buy into the worldview that work is not meant to be enjoyed. Nuts to that! You spend most of your life working, so if you don't enjoy it, that means you're not going to enjoy most of your life.

Also, crazy enough, the people I have run across who actually enjoy their work usually do the best work. Wild, right? They bring the most to the job because they like the job the most.

So I do think we need to strive to find a good fit for our strengths, values, and skill set so that we can do work we were made to do.

Just like you wouldn't want a mechanic performing brain surgery on you, and you wouldn't want a brain surgeon replacing the transmission in your car. I don't want my whiz-at-sales doing accounting. And I don't want my whiz-at-numbers designing my website. I want people who are good at what they do, doing what they do best.

Sometimes you are going to have to work some lousy jobs to get there, sure. I know I did. But sometimes you'll also learn the most about the work you want to do when embedded in work you like the least. Nothing can motivate a person more to find work they enjoy than when they are doing a job they strongly dislike. That, or they give up and do that job for the next forty years because, hey, work is not meant to be enjoyed so I'll stay in this dead yet comfortable place that doesn't require anything of me. At least they refilled the big glass bowl of chocolates in the front lobby!

NEXT STEPS:

- Let's be honest with ourselves about where we're working hard and where we're wasting time. Working hard is consistent, persistent, diligent work. If we keep tricking ourselves that we're doing good work when we're not, what are we ever going to work toward?

LIE #17
I don't have the time

When we say we don't have the time, what we really mean is, "It was not important enough for me to find the time."

For example, I'm guessing you've texted, called, or emailed someone, then about three weeks later you get a message back from them that basically says something like, "I'm sorry I didn't respond, but I've been so slammed with work and so busy I just didn't have the time."

I've received those messages and I've sent those messages. And of course it's not true. Because in the time we "didn't have," we spent lots of it aimlessly scrolling through social media. Watching Netflix shows. Taking a walk. Eating lunch. Waiting for a plane. There was tons of time to carve out a one-minute response.

Time wasn't the problem. Importance was.

Because if they would've texted you with a message saying, "Hey, I've got an extra ticket to (insert your favorite band or sporting event here)," you probably would have not only made the time to respond but also shifted all your plans around to make time to go with them, right?

Why do I bring this up? Is it basically to publicly out myself and all the apologetic messages I've sent? No. It's to remind all of us that it's not a question of time. It's a question of importance. If it's important to you, you will find the time.

We use this same excuse of not having the time when it comes to pursuing our dream. We all have to work. We all have to pay bills. Most times, for most people, that work isn't exactly what you want to do for the rest of your life. But I'd argue you *do* have time to work on your dream while still working at your job. It's not easy, but it's possible.

Time is a hot commodity in your twenties. You have more of it now than you probably will ever have again. Because each new step up you take on the "adulthood" ladder takes away a chunk of your time. Dating someone seriously or getting married means you now spend more time with them. Getting a promotion means more time working on the job. Having kids means they will try to find every reason imaginable to take up every second imaginable.

I can speak to this quite accurately as I try to write a book while also being a husband and a father of an eight-year-old, seven-year-old, three-year-old, and nine-month-old.

Time is split in so many ways now that I have no idea what time it is.

Make time for what is important. If you're having trouble figuring that out, ask yourself, "Is this my dream or is this a distraction?" If it's a distraction, move on to what's important.

Earl Nightingale, known as the Dean of Personal Development, years ago stated that if you read for an hour every day in your field of interest, you will become a top expert in three years. In five years, a national authority. In seven years, one of the best people in the world at what you do.

String wise hours together.

Stack wise days on top of one another.

You will be amazed at what you start building, in due time.

NEXT STEPS:

- Make a list of your top priorities in life. For me it's my faith, family, relationships, work, whole-being health, which includes finding some time to get into nature and home projects like gardening and building. Am I spending the right amount of time with these priorities or am I skewing too far to the extreme in one area? If I'm honest, I know I'll write down that my faith is a priority to me, yet I'll spend three minutes during the day praying and three hours in my yard working on growing new grass. Where I'm spending my time is telling me what I really deem as important more than what I say is important.

- Who is important to you in your life? Are you being intentional about making time for them? Then on the flipside, who are you giving too much time to that you shouldn't be? Making priorities in your relationships will help you spend that time wisely.

LIE #18

God, or the universe, is against me

We want to charge forward, yet we feel stuck. We feel pinned down and in pain. We want to live a good life, yet our current reality feels so lacking.

We start wondering if God has forgotten us. Or worse, if God is the one holding us down.

Pinned Down out of Love

I think about this as I reflect on a very intense week in my own life. My sweet little ten-month-old baby girl who just started walking tried to follow her three-year-old brother who had run down the stairs. Before anyone could catch up to her, she stepped off, not knowing the truth of gravity that was now at play. She crashed down the stairs and cried hysterically at the bottom.

It could've been much worse. Yet, she was still in pain because she had broken her arm.

First came the splint where the doctor, in his own words, learned about the "freakish strength" of this sweet little ten-month-old girl. It took two doctors plus my wife and me holding her down so they could put a splint on. Then a week later, even more fun, as now came the cast. We warned the doctor that she was stronger than she looked. The doctor quickly moved on to the task at hand, clearly having heard the same thing from parents before. Then after fifteen minutes of trying to wrap a cast and get it to settle, while this baby fought so hard she could've lifted up a Nissan Maxima, they had to start all over.

Now four of us again. And this is the image, the feeling I can't get out of my mind. I'm firmly pinning my beloved baby girl to a cold mat with my wife and two strangers. Our baby is in pain. She's afraid and crying hysterically. I'm holding her head down and her left arm as she screams, tears rolling down her cheeks, her head soaked in sweat from her intense struggle. She does not give up. She fights the entire time during the elongated process. I'm watching a cast dry on my baby as she looks at me with wild, questioning eyes that seem to say, "I thought you loved me!"

That's the image I can't get out of my mind. My heart feels ripped into tiny pieces as I think about it. I'm there right in front of her face, trying to calm her, trying to explain to her that this is for her best. That this is for her healing. That if we don't do this, her arm might never work correctly and she will continue to break it over and over as she crawls and falls. But in that moment, she doesn't understand any of it. She won't understand any of it until years later when we tell her the story. But we are pinning her down out of love. It's breaking my heart, but in spite of the pain and confusion on her face, what we're doing is saving her from a much deeper pain later.

Makes Me Lie Down

There's this well-known passage in the Bible that I've never really understood until now. It's talking about God . . .

> The LORD is my shepherd, I lack nothing.
> He makes me lie down in green pastures,
> he leads me beside quiet waters,
> he refreshes my soul.

> He guides me along the right paths
>> for his name's sake.
> Even though I walk
>> through the darkest valley,
> I will fear no evil,
>> for you are with me;
> your rod and your staff,
>> they comfort me.[1]

He "makes me" lie down in green pastures. I never understood that. It seemed too forceful. A juxtaposition of force and peace. If he "makes me" lie down in green pastures, how is that loving?

Well, I feel like I understand it more now, as I made my baby girl go through pain for her own healing. What feels like God's hate. Or what feels like God's aloofness or silence. Maybe God isn't punishing us or afflicting us. Maybe he's just forcing us to lie down in green pastures to refresh our souls. Maybe he's teaching us to trust him in the meadow and drink from the stream now. To rest now. To seek healing now. So that we can have the strength and faith to walk through the dark valley later.

I was not being an abusive father by willfully contributing to my daughter's pain and discomfort. It was because of my unending, undying love for her. I would've been a terrible parent if I hadn't taken her to the doctor and instead let her fall on her broken arm time and time again.

Sometimes healing doesn't feel very comfortable. Sometimes healing feels quite the opposite. Anyone who has gone through physical therapy and the excruciating pain of healing through intense struggle knows this principle all too well. I remember when I dislocated my shoulder in football and the pain that came from a little rubber band and trying to move it a few feet.

Sometimes the pain we feel now is our pathway out of death. Maybe God isn't holding us back. Maybe he's keeping us from falling off the ledge that we can't see in front of us.

As I see my baby daughter walking around now with a smile on her face, and she falls on her broken arm, she does not shriek in pain. Because she has a purple cast shield around her arm, protecting it, and that fills my heart with joy. She doesn't understand any of it now. But she will later.

NEXT STEPS:

- Are there any ways you've blamed God, or the universe, for something happening or not happening in your life? Why are we so quick to blame God? Do you think we can see the full picture clearly enough to accurately place blame?
- How many times have we blamed someone or something for a hard season in our lives when we were the ones making the bad decisions and then reaping the repercussions of them?
- I don't want to make light of what you've gone through, but hindsight can help us see a lot. When I look back at some painful seasons of my life where I felt like God was absent, I can see now that he was there; I just didn't see it at the time. I was stuck on all the "supposed to's" that I felt weren't happening instead of the blessings that were. The next lie I'll touch on is a powerful example of just this.

LIE #19

Nothing good can come out of this

Two sisters entered their new "home" knowing all too well that they'd most likely be killed there. A horrific thought, but an honest one.

They entered a massive room filled with rows and rows of wooden bunks stacked three high, nearly to the ceiling, with little room to walk in between. The windows throughout had large gaping holes where glass should've been—an unnerving sight, considering it was the dead of winter.

The two sisters climbed up and crawled back to their second-tier bunk—a platform they would share with other women—and lay in the straw-covered bed that reeked of urine and mold.

Corrie ten Boom stared silently at the ceiling and wondered how she could survive a day in this Nazi concentration camp. She and her sister Betsie were Dutch Christians, arrested for suspicion of harboring Jewish "fugitives." An allegation that was definitely true, even if the Nazi Security Service never found any of the six people hidden in a secret, strategically constructed upstairs closet.[1]

As Corrie pondered her fate, she felt something bite her. She popped up, hitting her head on the wooden slats. Corrie and her sister Betsie clamored down off their bunk to escape, their bodies covered with fleas.

Everything taken from them, now living in one of the most horrific, evil places in history—their chance of survival was as likely as getting the guards to transport them to a penthouse suite. How could they live in such a place?

Betsie had the answer, something she remembered from a Bible verse they had read that morning. She knew that was the only way they could make it. Her audacious survival strategy? To give thanks. For *everything* about their new lives.

As Corrie described when recounting a conversation she had with her sister, she wasn't quite sure this constant thankfulness was even possible.

I stared at her, then around me at the dark, foul-aired room.
"Such as?" I said.
"Such as being assigned here together."
I bit my lip. "Oh yes, Lord Jesus!"
"Such as what you're holding in your hands."
I looked down at the Bible. "Yes! Thank You, dear Lord, that there was no inspection when we entered here! Thank You for all the women, here in this room, who will meet You in these pages."
"Yes," said Betsie. "Thank You for the very crowding here. Since we're packed so close, that many more will hear!" She looked at me expectantly. "Corrie!" she prodded.
"Oh, all right. Thank You for the jammed, crammed, stuffed, packed, suffocating crowds."
"Thank You," Betsie went on serenely, "for the fleas and for—"
The fleas! This was too much. "Betsie, there's no way even God can make me grateful for a flea."
"'Give thanks in all circumstances,'" she quoted. "It doesn't say, 'in pleasant circumstances.' Fleas are part of this place where God has put us."[2]

Corrie was sure this time Betsie had officially lost her mind.

Months in Hell and the Unexpected Amazing

For weeks and months they worked and survived in a place that was just a quick escalator ride up from hell itself.

Yet, an amazing thing began to happen.

Quite timidly, at nights while soup was being served, Corrie and Betsie started reading from their Bible aloud in the back of the massive dormitory room as women gathered around to listen.

They would read the Dutch text and then translate it to German, then listen as women repeated the words back through the crowd in French, Russian, Polish, and Czech. It was ripples of hope and light being spoken in a place all too absent of both.

Reading the Bible was illegal in this place. With guards everywhere, Corrie and Betsie feared being discovered and the horrific fate that would await them if they were. Yet, night after night they continued uninterrupted. The gatherings became so big that Corrie and Betsie held two church services a night in the dormitory. Women being filled with courage and strength to face what awaited them at 3:30 a.m. when they would be cattle-prodded out of bed for work duty the next day.

How many lives were Corrie and Betsie saving?

Every night they feared a guard would discover them, yet it was like God put a protective force field around them. Then one day they figured out the truth of what God's protective force field was all along. They figured out what allowed them to carry out their illegal act of giving hope every night to women who were in desperate need of it.

The protective force field?

The infestation of the fleas.

They discovered that no guard wanted to take a step into their dormitory lest they got fleas themselves. As Betsie shared her news of the flea revelation with Corrie, she couldn't help but shine an "I told you so" smile. *See, there was a reason to be thankful for the fleas.*

Insanely, audaciously thankful.

Being thankful for the blessings of life is easy. Being thankful for the crap, the setbacks, the "why is this happening to me?" is another.

Yet, it's being thankful for the stuff we can't see that's a good reason to be thankful for that which might be the most transformative.

Because we don't see the full picture. We can't read our entire story from where we currently sit. We don't know how the obstacles and turns and failures and confusion and setbacks and struggles are coming together to create our future.

I often look back at past events that I was sure were massive mistakes and failures, and how they led to something more substantial. Sometimes the events in our life that are not necessarily easy are the most necessary.

I've learned over the years, mainly while complaining and grumbling, that my amazing plans weren't that amazing to begin with. Only by my wonderful plans going up in flames could a better, more substantial plan be put in its place.

I'm still trying to learn that sometimes it's those annoying fleas of life that end up saving me.

Betsie ten Boom wouldn't survive the holocaust camp during WWII, but her hope and vision would inspire her sister Corrie to keep fighting and find a way out, sharing their story in one of the most powerful books I've ever read: *The Hiding Place*.

Also, in an unbelievable collection of events, Corrie continued Betsie's vision for creating a massive postwar mansion that would be a place of healing for those brutalized by the war—both for the victims and for those who had inflicted the pain. Corrie carried on Betsie's calling and character of healing and thankfulness, even to the very same Nazis who had helped kill her sister. An unbelievable act of reconciliation and healing.

Most times we can't see the full picture. Can we give thanks for the parts that have yet to be revealed? How would that change our perspective and our lives if we did?

What would happen if we found purpose and redemption, not in spite of the pain, but smack dab in the fleshy wound of it?

As Nobel Prize–winning author and fellow Holocaust survivor Elie Wiesel wrote: "No one is as capable of gratitude as one who has emerged from the kingdom of night."[3]

When you've really been through it, you're really thankful when you get out of it. When you've experienced the kingdom of night, you want to be sunlight so others don't have to experience the same darkness.

The Ten Boom Perspective

Maybe you've seen some of this play out in your life while going through the COVID-19 pandemic (and I really hope COVID-20 or COVID-anything is not a thing when you're reading this). While I haven't gone through nearly the experience that the Ten Boom sisters did, I've definitely found myself being much more thankful and appreciative of so many daily parts of life during and (hopefully) after COVID-19 that I so easily took for granted before.

Seeing friends. Talking to friends. A hug or a handshake. Taking a walk or going on a bike ride. Sitting in a coffee shop. The reaffirmed truth of what a luxury a grocery store is. Sharing experiences with others, like a baseball game or a concert. Health—for me, and especially for my family. Clean water. A roof over my head. All the amazing, hardworking people in this world who keep it running. I have a fresh perspective of the miracle that each one of these things are.

> Every experience God gives us . . . is the perfect preparation for the future only He can see.
>
> —Corrie ten Boom

When things start getting stripped away in life, we begin to realize how many blessings we have. And maybe those failed plans, lost expectations, and hurts of the past don't carry with them the same sting as before. Because we have a clearer perspective of what really matters. Those problems that felt all-consuming before don't crush us as much now. Like the fleas that Betsie ten Boom was able to thank God for—a nuisance and discomfort that was keeping a much greater evil from entering into their "home."

NEXT STEPS:

- Can you look at any painful or frustrating events in your lives and see them with "Ten Boom perspective"? Were there any paradigm shifts in your thinking that took place as a result? A truth that was learned or reinforced? A hope that was created? A passion that was discovered? An opportunity that was opened? The start of something good?
- Could the painful event have been much worse, but something took place like the fleas in the Holocaust camp that became a refuge of sorts?

LIE #20

Finding my worth through what is "social media worthy"

My wife was scrolling through various mom-fluencers' Instagram accounts. Always the student looking for patterns and connections, my wife made an announcement to me.

"I've discovered the secret," she said seriously. "I know how these moms get the most likes."

"Alright, I'll bite," I said, looking up from my book. "What's the secret?"

"Matching outfits," she responded.

"Matching outfits?" I asked.

"Yes. They get all the kids in matching outfits. Sometimes the wife and husband too. Those are the posts that get the most likes." She nodded. "So not surprisingly, they match a lot."

I'm not sure if she was just reporting her findings or floating the idea out there for our family's next-step brand-building integrated Instagram matching-outfit strategy. All I could think about was—what are these parents bribing (or sedating) their kids with to pull off their matching outfit of smiling ensconced in a perfectly decorated room that feels worthy of the last two minutes of *Fixer Upper*?

For us, just trying to get all four kids in the picture where one child is not pulling the hair of the other or someone is not looking like they want to break the phone in two across their knee is a picture worthy of a Christmas card.

Now, not only are we subjected to scrolling through the amazingness of our friends' kids/pets, exotic travels, OMG achievements, and food pics, now every third post is a Sponsored Post! What a blessing. Now, I have a new way to be advertised to whilst feeling terrible about my career as some "expert" shares their "can't miss formula" for "getting more clients, making more money, starting something with marginal success" so that one day you can also run sponsored posts to help others do the same.

I don't think it's a problem that we're posting pictures of our lives on social media. I think it becomes a problem when we're constantly looking at our lives through the lens of "Is this social media worthy?" Then when the answer, in our opinion, is a possible no, we start figuring out a way to make it so. Kids in matching outfits! Check. Spur-of-the-moment, whimsical selfie that took me an hour, and fifty different photos to get to make sure no one could see my double chin, and then I write some inspiring caption to go with it about the meaning of life to cover up the fact that I really just wanted to post this good-looking, "impromptu" picture of myself, because I worked so hard to make it happen.

Or some darker consequences. Like going for that extreme selfie of your hike up to the waterfall and then falling off the cliff. "Selfie-related injuries and deaths" are a real thing, with lots of data on Wikipedia.

Or my wife, Naomi, and I knew a couple where the wife was obsessed with wanting to build her Instagram page with exotic travel photos. This meant spending thousands and thousands of dollars on trips. I think they went on something like seven big trips their first year of marriage. Her obsession with Instagram became one of the biggest reasons they got divorced.

Or you kind of just keep everyone at arm's length from actually seeing you and your real life by continually posting pictures that make your life look amazing, when secretly it doesn't feel that way at all. You never feel like you can be honest, because then people will see you for the "fake" you are. You start needing the likes. They become like a drug. Giving you a high or low, depending on how successful the social media hit was.

Or you become depressed because your life feels not social media worthy whatsoever, so you never want to post anything. Yet, you spend hours enviously looking through the social-media-worthy lives of others. Like you're standing in the corner of the party, not talking to anyone, yet becoming more and more bitter at all the "cool kids" there who seemingly have it all. Who don't actually have it all, they're just the best at faking it like they do.

Where is our worth coming from? Has social media become a daily death by validation?

I want my kids to live good lives. Full lives. Healthy lives, where they know how beautiful and talented they are. Where they can see their worth and ability like their parents can. Social media feels like the last thing in the world I want them to be a part of. Why would I want that for them? For me? For you?

I empathize with middle schoolers, high schoolers, and college students now as they grow up in this social media immersion. Because when I had rough seasons in school, with acne, braces, and insecurities galore, I could leave the walls and bullies of high school and find refuge back home. Now, especially if the student is on social media, there is no escape. The bullies can enter into their bedroom with just one quick, poisonous comment online. We're afraid to let kids ride bikes around the neighborhood for fear that something bad might happen, and yet, we let the dangers of the world have direct access to them in their own bedrooms on some device?

What good is all this constant social media-ing bringing us? What picture of success and contentment are all these images showing us? What is the question "Is this social media worthy?"

138

doing to our real worth? When you post something, how often do you check the post to see how many likes you have? If you don't have many, do you start feeling depressed? Even if you have a lot, is it ever enough?

Do you scroll through "influencer" or celebrity social media accounts and leave feeling better about the place you're in and what you have in life? Or do you now feel lacking and insignificant?

What typically gets higher social media engagement? Is it the meaningful, quiet, and humble moments of life? Or is it the loud, highly filtered, brash, argumentative, angry, lewd, or silly? Social media engagement can't be our barometer of success. There are plenty of posts that have high social media engagement and very low actual worth and meaning to the world.

Do you know your worth? Or are you posting on social media to have your worth validated? Are you encouraging others to find theirs through social media?

Are you worthy without social media's validation?

NEXT STEPS:

- Have you tried answering some of the questions I asked above? Give it a shot. Then, go back to your last ten social media posts—are you posting from a place of worth and meaning or are you posting hoping to find worth and meaning? Are you posting to help others be seen and heard, or are you shouting to be seen and heard? Are you validating the worth of others or are you desperately hoping to be validated? Are you seeing your worth through the lens of social media? If so, your worth will be on a roller coaster of highs and lows.
- Instead of using the amount of likes as the barometer for success for a post, we should ask, "What worth did I bring

to the world with this post?" If it feels like you brought something meaningful—laughter, guidance, encouragement, wisdom, a hand up, reassurance, etc.—then it's a successful post no matter how many or few likes you receive.

LIE #21

I'm well-informed

We have a glut of information.

But do we have a glut of wisdom? Gleaning rich information and applying it in the right way at the right time.

If the answer feels like a no, which it does to me, why is that the case?

What's the main source of our information today and through what medium? Well, for most of us, it's our phone, right? Information cascading to us through the internet. But there's just too much. So it's condensed for us by what's trending, what's hot, what people are sharing on social media, what we want to see based on what we've clicked on before. It's headlines, quick snippets, algorithms catered to personally serve and appease us throughout our day, all day, every day.

In an article by Trevor Haynes and Rebecca Clements for Harvard, they state that "adults in the US spend an average of 2–4 hours per day tapping, typing, and swiping on their devices—that adds up to over 2,600 daily touches."[1]

Have you started receiving your weekly summary of your phone usage? I have. It's depressing. I'm right there in those stats above. Every time I see it, I think it must be wrong. There's no way I'm on the phone that much, I argue with my phone while I stare at it.

"I feel tremendous guilt," said Chamath Palihapitiya, former Vice President of User Growth at Facebook to an audience of Stanford students. He was responding to a question about his involvement in exploiting consumer behavior. "The short-term, dopamine-driven feedback loops that we have created are destroying how society works. No civil discourse, no cooperation, misinformation, mistruth and it's not an American problem. This is a global problem. It is eroding the core foundations of how people behave by and between each other."[2]

Author, activist, and Trappist monk Thomas Merton has these pointed words about the internet and social media that he wrote in his collection *Confessions of a Guilty Bystander*. It is so on point that I felt I needed to quote it in its entirety:

> This is one of the few real pleasures left to modern man: this illusion that he is thinking for himself when, in fact, someone else is doing his thinking for him. And this someone else is not a personal authority, the great mind of a genial thinker, it is the mass mind, the general "they," the anonymous whole. One is left, therefore, not only with the sense that one has thought things out for himself, but he has reached the correct answer without difficulty—the answer which is shown to be correct because it is the answer of everybody. Since it is at once my answer and the answer of everybody, how should I resist?[3]

His statement is a lot to take in, but I feel there's so much truth in it about the internet and social media that it was especially pertinent to discuss here. Except, I've lied to you a bit (in my book about lies!). Thomas Merton did not write this observation about social media and the internet. This quote was published in his book in 1966, and Merton would tragically die in 1968. What Merton was describing was not social media or the internet. What he was describing was the ill effects of using propaganda! Merton would die long before the internet and social media were even remote realities.

I found it incredibly interesting, and slightly terrifying, that Merton's spot-on description of propaganda could also be a spot-on critique of our use of the internet and social media.

Typically, when I think of propaganda, I think of World War II, of the messages, movies, and posters being made on all sides of the war, demonizing the enemy. Propaganda is usually synonymous with the Nazi party and Joseph Goebbels, who was put in the prominent position by his friend Adolph Hitler to be minister for public "enlightenment" and propaganda. An alarmingly paradoxical title, if you ask me. Goebbels would be responsible for helping steer an entire nation to some of the most horrible atrocities of humankind.

Propaganda, as defined by Lexico, is "information, especially of a biased or misleading nature, used to promote or publicize a particular political cause or point of view." The illusion of thinking for ourselves when the general "they" is giving us the answer that we already thought was the answer so of course it must be true.

The question is sitting there, staring at me, and I feel it must be asked: How much of the information that we are receiving via social media and the internet is "accurate" information, trying its best to enlighten the population with a well-articulated discussion of truth on a given subject? And how much of the information we see is heightened, dramatic, sensationalized, one-sided "biased or misleading" information? Or, in other words, propaganda.

I mean, if we take out "biased and misleading information" from social media and the internet, I'm not sure we'd have social media. We'd have like one headline a day.

Is social media merely becoming a platform of socially acceptable propaganda that is thinking for us while it pats us on the back for thinking for ourselves?

Factfulness and the Internet

Through decades of research and in his book *Factfulness*, Hans Rosling, an international public health expert and professor, presents strong evidence that most of us are completely off when it comes to our view of the world. When Rosling would ask questions about the state of the world, even to rooms full of the smartest people in the world, they received shockingly low scores. Even a chimpanzee picking answers at random would "consistently outguess teachers, journalists, Nobel laureates, and investment bankers."[4]

Usually people's answers have one thing in common—they see the world as much worse off than it *actually* is. When you look at this data from the perspective of where most of us are receiving our information from, it's not surprising that we think the world is one step away from all-out WWIII nuclear war every day. Because the more emotional your headline, the more likely it will be shared.[5]

Or as the researchers behind the study "Good Friends, Bad News—Affect and Virality in Twitter" described regarding the most shared and engaged tweets on Twitter: "Our findings may be summarized 'If you want to be cited: Sweet talk your friends or serve bad news to the public.'"[6]

As Hans Rosling sums up succinctly in *Factfulness*: "Every group of people I ask thinks the world is more frightening, more violent, and more hopeless—in short, more dramatic—than it really is. . . . Westerners [especially] have an overdramatic world-view. It's stressful and misleading."[7]

We think we've got the facts down. We think we aren't swayed by biased, emotional information. Yet, the data shows that's not the case.

Filter Bubbles and the Internet

Author, researcher, and entrepreneur Eli Pariser coined the phrase "filter bubble" when referring to the way we are receiving highly tailored information on the internet, programmed just for us. In Pariser's TED Talk "Beware of Online Filter Bubbles," he quoted former Google CEO Eric Schmidt, who stated: "It will be very hard for people to watch or consume something that has not in some sense been tailored for them."[8]

The irony was not lost on me that, after listening to this TED Talk about the danger of only taking in information tailored specifically to what we want to hear, I would go to the TED Talks website where I would be directed to a landing page with a big title in the middle—

TED Recommends
Talks recommended just for you, delivered to your inbox
What interests you?

Apparently TED did not take their talks' own advice.

Confirmation Bias and the Internet

You've probably heard the term *confirmation bias* before and the psychological studies that have been done around this mental phenomenon. Basically, confirmation bias is "when we have formed a view, we embrace information that confirms that view while ignoring, or rejecting, information that casts doubt on it."[9]

Again, it's not hard to see confirmation bias as a bedrock foundation to social media, especially in light of the algorithms used to tailor the information to us based on our preferences. So, let's say you have a certain disposition toward a political candidate. The views that you're going to see on social media are most likely going to be confirmation of what you already believe to be the truth about that person—whether positive or negative. The bias gets confirmed without much conscious thought that you've never fully explored opinions or evidence from the other side. Why should you? What you "know" to be true was shown to you to be exactly right.

Yet, it's not just the internet that can do this. We can receive propaganda from real live people as well. I often fear the college campus can quickly become a place of biased and sensationalized views, not based on facts, but based on a fuming anger toward the other party, whichever side that is.

We must question who is giving us the answer. We must look at the fruit of the source.

Thinking on the Internet

No matter the medium of information, we are all going to have biased opinions based on a litany of experiences and values that we hold true, even if we do not realize it. But it is in the feedback loops, echo chambers, sensationalized headlines, infotainment, the way in which the biased opinions are being shown to us based off what Google or whatever social media platform's algorithms say we are biased toward. We have to examine how we are taking in this information and basing our entire worldview on it.

Yet, here I am, doing research about the bias of the internet, by doing research on the internet.

Is any of what I'm saying ringing true or was I being fed some lie by some algorithmic search?

Well, I guess it comes down to our intentionality, our choices, our ability to hunt down truth with the same resourcefulness we would've done finding and cross-referencing sources in a library. Will we strive to think on our own and use the tools in front of us in our search? Will we try to seek out information from both sides? Or will we let the tools make the decision for us, without any thought whatsoever that the tools can actually do that?

But I will tell you, back to the Thomas Merton quote above, I stumbled across it while drinking coffee at my stay at the Downing House, a quiet place of spiritual, intellectual retreat. I've stayed here three nights as I've worked on this book. When I stumbled across that quote, hidden on page 238, written by a Trappist monk over fifty years ago, and it struck me as a perfect description of the downsides of the internet and social media by a man who didn't know the internet would even exist, it felt like I was discovering a message in a bottle. I felt a certain excitement, like I had discovered a truth I didn't know I would find. Like hidden treasure.

I didn't press a button in the book and ask it to give me its thoughts about propaganda. I had to dive into it. I had to read other pages that I didn't connect with. I had to concentrate. I had to read those lines about propaganda and then use my own thinking to make the connection to social media. The spark and excitement of an original idea. It was an exploration of sorts where I dug into the ground and found a nugget of gold.

It was learning and thinking without an algorithm to guide me. It was learning and thinking far beyond what I thought I would be learning and thinking about. Maybe that's the most profound learning of all.

It wasn't streamlined. It wasn't efficient. I felt like I was thinking about it in a way no one else in the world was at that moment. It felt magical—like I was having a conversation with Thomas Merton in his small hermitage as I smelled the coffee he was drinking. Not just reading the bullet-point highlights of his life but experiencing it without anyone telling me what I should be experiencing.

The fact that you're reading this book right now is that same sort of magic, isn't it? You are exploring. You are seeking truth and wisdom beyond what you thought you knew. Sure, some of this book won't ring true for you. I get that. Maybe it will in a few years. Maybe not at all.

You probably even had an expectation of what this book would be before you started reading, and one of two things is happening. I'm either joyfully exceeding that expectation for you, or I've missed that expectation by 100 miles and you will let me, and the world, know about that in a quite lengthy review ripping every piece of my book and being to shreds.

But by being brave enough to explore, and making a sacrifice to read, you are doing something near revolutionary today. Whether this book has been a joy or a struggle for you to read, you're still here. You're in it. That's amazing. You're thinking—and that, today, is a courageous and freeing act that no internet algorithm can control.

Man with the Crooked Staff

All of this might be overstated. Maybe this place of quiet retreat has me thinking in a different age, like I've become the old man on the hill with the long gray beard and crooked wooden staff, yelling to anyone who will listen.

Don't get me wrong, I don't want to do away with advancements in technology. But I do want to think critically about how I'm using them and how I want my kids to use them.

We all need to honestly look at our information intake through the lens of filter bubbles, confirmation bias, "factfulness," infotainment, and the overwhelming glut of information that the internet offers. Getting information is easy these days. Getting the right information that becomes knowledge and wisdom is really hard. How do we know what is true and what is false?

Am I always thinking for myself? No, I'm not. That's the truth. But I sure want to think more about the ways I can.

NEXT STEPS:

- How do we become more well-informed? Well, let's start by reading more books. This has been a quality answer for being a more well-informed person since Gutenberg was spinning the wheels on that first printing press. And hey, you're doing just that! Well done. Keep going. There are so many good books out there. Not sure where to start? I have an article on allgroanup.com on the 27 must-read books for your twenties. These books were the most influential to me in my twenties, like *Man's Search for Meaning, Let Your Life Speak*, and *War of Art*. I also love reading history books because it gives me a context and understanding for where we've been and what we're going through today.

- While not all books are good and the authors will still have their biases, books typically have a lot more checks and balances to go through during the writing and creation process to make sure the information is sound, solid, and factual.

- If there's a topic or current event you really are intrigued by, then read a few books or various articles on the subject, but include some that are coming to the subject from different sides. You have to do the work of a reporter, checking sources against each other to see which seems the least biased and most objective.

- Also try to stretch yourself by reading books on topics you're not naturally drawn to.

- Another get-informed action step beyond books is talking to real people who are working in the field you find yourself talking about the most. I wonder how many people who constantly go to war online about politics have sat down with a politician from either side to better understand who they are and what they do.

- And one last idea of being more well-informed: meeting and talking to people who are smarter than you. Meet with these people and be intentional about asking the person good questions.

LIE #22

It needs to be perfect

> Perfect? That's the devil. They should strike the damn thing
> out of the language of the human race.
>
> —Sam Phillips, record producer

You ever heard of Sam Phillips before? How about Elvis Presley or Johnny Cash? Well, that's like asking if you've ever heard of the United States. Those last guys alone probably shaped the blurred lines of American music more than anyone else. How about piano prodigy Jerry Lee Lewis and his songs like "Great Balls of Fire"? B.B. King? Ike Turner? Roy Orbison (most known for the song "Pretty Woman")? Howlin' Wolf? The list goes on and on.

I'm not listing these artists to try and un-impress you with my 1960s who's who of music. I'm listing all these artists because in one shape or another they were discovered by one lone record producer who operated a tiny storefront, independent record label called Sun Records in Memphis, Tennessee.

As a big Johnny Cash fan, I was excited to learn more about the producer who helped discover him, in the excellent book *Sam Phillips: The Man Who Invented Rock 'n' Roll* by Peter Guralnick. Not only did this record producer, Sam Phillips, cultivate some of the most influential musicians of the twentieth century, he helped change the course of music forever by ushering in a new frontier of music that slowly began to be called "rock 'n' roll." Sam Phillips might be more influential to music than any of the artists above. And as a huge Johnny Cash fan myself (and with the millions of Elvis groupies and impersonators who still canvass this earth), that's saying a lot!

So how did Sam Phillips pull this off, most of it while in his twenties and early thirties? What was his secret?

Well, first he had a lot of empathy and a lack of prejudice that allowed him to see the world differently than most. Growing up in the south in a poor farming community he could see a movement, he saw an undercurrent trend, a "blue ocean" just waiting to be explored that few else had seen. It was the heart, soul, pain, and truth of the south through the voices of Black musicians. And it broke his heart that there wasn't a place for these musicians to record, to share their music with White and Black audiences alike. He felt like the beauty and truth of music could break through the barriers of discrimination more than anything else.[1]

So his studio was an open door, and he'd listen to anyone who came in to sing. Then to make ends meet, Sam was also hustling, recording anything that somebody would pay him for, whether it was running the sound at a local baseball park, or Sam's big entrepreneurial idea—teaming up with a funeral home to offer people a recording of their loved one's service.

Slowly musicians started trickling in. Whether they could barely play an instrument or were so nervous they could hardly get a word out, Sam Phillips would sit patiently and encourage the person in front of him to just give it a try. To let their voice be heard through only the way they could sing it.

Take, for example, a poor, shy teenager who came in to record a few songs as a gift to his mom. While this boy's voice was unpolished with many flaws, there was something about the honesty and ache in his tone that kept playing in Sam's mind. A year later he heard a song that he thought might be a good fit for this boy, so he brought in two musicians to see if they could record it. And it was a downright failure. The boy just couldn't quite seem to get the song down. So they tried another song and another, each time failing to come together. But Sam just kept encouraging them to give it another shot and, in his trademark philosophy for recording, make it fun. If it wasn't fun, then what was the point?

Sam would run the recording sessions in a completely uncontrolled manner. He didn't want it to be forced. He wanted the musicians to keep trying, keep reaching, keep extending themselves past their own insecurities and fears that were holding them back, and just sing the way only they could sing.

Well, with this recording session now stretching into early morning, Sam started packing up. Maybe they could give it a shot another day. That's when this young teenage boy just started "acting a fool" with a song he'd heard a while back, with the other two musicians jumping in and slapping their instruments in excitement.

Sam heard it, and now he knew he'd *really* heard something. Backed up in a corner, about to be sent home, this young singer just gave it a "What the heck" kind of performance, and that night they ended up recording "That's All Right (Mama)," Elvis's first recording. And within only weeks, a smashing success unlike anything Sun Records had ever experienced. That night shy, unassuming, little-known Elvis of Memphis, Tennessee, became Elvis Presley.

As Sam Phillips repeatedly said, "I love perfect imperfection, I really do, and that's not just some cute saying, that's a fact."[2]

It's in the awkward. It's in the discomfort. It's when you have your back up against the wall, so you say, "What the heck" and just LET IT RIP! That's where the real beauty lives and breathes. When you explore without any clear sense of where exactly you're supposed to end up. When you dive in without any clear idea how you're going to get out. Sam wasn't looking for musicians who sounded like what was playing on the radio. Sam was looking for musicians who sounded like themselves. Sam was looking for something raw and authentic.

That's what attracted him to another musician who stumbled in with two mechanics struggling to be musicians who could barely play a whole song through. But there was something about the simplicity in which they played that became its own thing. There was something about the honesty and rhythm of the singer's voice that seemed to cut through like a train. There was something about this struggling door-to-door salesman and the honesty of his songs "Cry! Cry! Cry!" and "Folsom Prison Blues" that attracted Phillips to JR Cash. Not letting JR know he thought the name "Johnny" sounded better until JR "Johnny" saw it printed on his first record label.

Or as author Peter Guralnick put it, Sam tried to make every record as perfect as it could be. Not perfect in the usual, conventional terms, but perfect on its own terms. What Sam was after was *"perfection of feeling*, not perfection of technique."[3]

Another Sun musician, Carl Perkins, who was good friends with Johnny Cash, was listening one night to Cash tell a story about being in the Air Force. Cash joked about all the guys wearing the standard black shoes, but when one guy got his foot stepped on, he joked, "Hey, get off my blue suede shoes."

Something about that line struck Carl Perkins. So that night he went home to the projects where he was barely scraping by with his wife and two kids. He went out on the front steps so as not to wake anyone. He dumped out potatoes from a brown paper sack, and on it he wrote the lyrics to "Blue Suede Shoes."

Perkins then stepped into the studio with his band, and he described the recording process like this.

"I'd say, 'Mr. Phillips, that's terrible.' He said, 'That's original.' I said, 'But it's just a big original mistake.' He said, 'That's what Sun Records is. That's what we are.'"[4]

"Blue Suede Shoes" and Carl Perkins would become Sun Records' first million-album seller way before Elvis would record his own version of "Blue Suede Shoes" and make the song his own.

Wading into the Unknown

I'm in the middle of writing this book, and quite a few people will ask me if I've outlined the entire book or if I know what I'm going to write. I just smile and tell them, "Honestly, I don't really have a clue."

I don't outline a book. I just start jotting down notes throughout the day. Any thought or idea that strikes me as interesting, funny, or memorable, I jot down. I have pages and pages of these notes. I don't know if they'll lead to anything or they'll lead to everything, or somewhere in between, but I let myself swim out into the water so that I have to fight to find the stuff that's going to keep me, and hopefully this book, afloat.

I'm not saying if you're structured or if you love a good concrete outline that you can't do good work. I'm just saying that we have to allow space for perfect imperfection to live and breathe. We have to set up a place, like Sam Phillips, where people, including ourselves, feel accepted to take that original risk. We'll gladly encourage others to be themselves and take that risk, while we ourselves cling tight to the end of the rope in fear of letting go.

We can follow all the recipes. Or we can work, fail, and stumble upon creating a few signature recipes of our own. We should become more comfortable with taking unchained chances.

> Those are my most favorite parts of this record, when we weren't going for perfect. We were going for the most vibe and most feeling.
>
> —Wesley Shultz, Lumineers lead singer when discussing their third album

Creating Your Own Reese's Peanut Butter Cup

Have you ever watched the YouTube video of musician and producer Pharrell Williams at the NYU Masterclass when he meets unknown NYU student Maggie Rogers?[5] Go watch it if you haven't. Basically, unknown musician Maggie Rogers sits down next to Pharrell, they play her song "Alaska," and the rest became history as her music career was launched into hyperdrive.

"I have zero . . . zero, zero notes for that," Pharrell says when the song ends and Maggie's face lights up with shock and amazement. "Because you're doing your own thing. It's singular."[6]

Pharrell then goes on to compare each one of our abilities to creating something like the peanut butter cup. Bringing two amazing things together to create a third, something amazing in its own way. As Pharrell states, you can hear that play out in Maggie's music. A singer-songwriter folk musician who also weaves in an electronic dance beat—two typically separate genres of music coming together to create her own "peanut butter cup."

Bring meaningful things together in a meaningful way that means something to you.

You have a unique ache and angle to your story that needs to be told. Many people will tell you otherwise. They'll tell you the clichés of toeing the line. Sure, learn the traditional techniques. Toe the line. Then jump.

It's the fail-proof formula: the more you put yourself in a very real position where you can fail, the better chance you have at creating something meaningful.

I think many of us are still searching for a formula from someone, anyone, so that we don't have to fail. We want the path. The steps. The answer. The hand to get us over every conceivable obstacle. We want the syllabus laid out in front of us again.

Yet, we can follow some "proven" formula perfectly and still fail miserably. It may even look like we haven't failed—the outcome might be just what the formula promised. But you've taken a shortcut to get where you thought you wanted to be. You gave up and started lying to yourself that you don't have what it takes to create something more, something meaningful outside of someone else's formula. By taking the safe route that promised no failure, you actually fall short of what *could have been* because you never ventured out. You never allowed yourself space to fail.

It's like going on a trail ride on horseback. You paid the money, sometimes quite literally, to follow the horse's rear end in front of you. You thought you were going out on a wild, beautiful ride. Instead, you go on a safe ride, in a big circle, ending right back in the same space as when you started.

Many of us are on that same ride. We might never take the risk of getting off the beaten path because we don't want to get lost. Yet now, on the same, safe path, falling in line with the others like we always have, we feel more lost than ever because we were never willing to risk exploring our own path. The safe path is not always the comfortable one.

All Explorers Have to Get Lost

Believe me, this is scary. This is unnerving. One day while working on this book, those lies that "I HAVE NOTHING MORE TO OFFER" were blaring across the loudspeakers in my mind. So I walked away from my computer and lay down in the grass. There I started really pleading to God for help: "I feel like I am trying to write this book in a dense fog. Help!"

Flat on my back, looking at the sky, I felt the answer come to me in my spirit.

"When you can't see, you actually have to trust me to guide you out. Maybe the point isn't to escape the fog. Maybe the point is to sit down in it. To feel it. To rest in it. To come to grips with it. And to understand the truth of it. When you can't see is when your other senses come alive. Listen. Feel. Smell. Trust. Don't rush to escape the fog. Maybe the fog is trying to show you something you couldn't have 'seen' without it."

We all want to do something memorable. But few of us will allow ourselves to enter that very real vortex of awkward where you're blindly finding your way. Where you're running into walls headfirst, yet with each crash, you're more clearly understanding where the openings are.

Listening to the Tape Backward

One of my favorite Johnny Cash songs is "Walk the Line," and it's one of the final songs he did with producer Sam Phillips. So simple, yet something about it is so unique. Johnny Cash tells the origin of the song coming from one night going to his shift at the Air Force base when he pressed play on a tape deck. What Johnny heard totally shocked and confused him. The sound coming from the speakers was unlike anything he'd ever heard. It almost seemed otherworldly, and at the end of the noises he heard what sounded like "Father." Then the tape shut off.

For months Johnny Cash listened to that tape during his shift. The sounds were so unique, so strange, he couldn't get them out of his head. Finally, curiosity got the best of him, and after months of listening, he took the tape out to inspect it further. That's when he realized that someone had put the tape in backward maybe as a joke or as a "happy little accident," and the otherworldly sounds he'd been hearing were simply someone strumming a guitar, then saying "Cut it off."

But Johnny Cash could not get those backward chord progressions sounds out of his head. He'd heard something truly unique and he really listened to it. So he wrote it into the melody and created the song "Walk the Line," which carries a unique chord progression unlike any country song before it. Or pop song. It was a song in its own category. Johnny Cash had to hum in between verses just to keep his pitch, giving it another unique Johnny Cash-ism that would make the song "singular."

Here's the best formula I can give you. Take the formula. Learn the formula. Rip up the formula. Create your own formula that is flexible enough to continually be re-created. But don't skip the step of learning the original formula or else you won't know how to build off of it.

It's allowing your ears and eyes to be open to sounds and sights you haven't heard before. You don't walk on the moon without the very real possibility that you ain't making it home.

As we set out on our own explorations, we have to strike "perfection" out of our vocabulary. It's never going to be the perfect time to start. It's never going to be the perfect idea. It's never going to be the perfect person to marry. Perfection is a lie.

Perfection is fear masquerading as good taste. Searching for perfection is a perfectly good way to never create or complete anything worth creating.

Sometimes we have to listen to the tape backward. Sometimes we need to experiment with putting peanut butter and chocolate together.

Sometimes we just need to dump out those potatoes from the sack and start writing on it. Sometimes we just have to take a step out into the unknown, and who knows, maybe we will stumble on a big, original mistake like Elvis Presley or Johnny Cash.

Perfect imperfection. Sam Phillips would be proud.

NEXT STEPS:

- Can you spot things in your life that you've been afraid to move forward into because you're waiting for it to be perfect? It will never be perfect nor is it supposed to. Walk forward. Walk the line! Sure you might stumble off it at points, but now you're moving forward. As Sam Phillips told author Peter Guralnick in *The Man Who Invented Rock 'n' Roll*: "If the best comes, fine. If it doesn't, don't be disappointed. Just make sure, wherever you get with your mission—make sure that up to that point, step by step, you were satisfied."[7]

LIE #23

What if it doesn't work out?

Do you remember when Conan O'Brien took over for Jay Leno as the host of *The Tonight Show*? It was Conan's dream come true, something he'd worked toward for sixteen years as the late-night host after Leno.

Then in seven months, Conan was gone. Replaced by Jay Leno. Sending Conan into a yearlong desert experience where everything he'd been working toward vanished.

It was Conan O'Brien's worst fear realized, and yet, it was also the catalyst to some of his greatest successes.

As Conan explained in a college graduation speech at Dartmouth University after his fallout with *The Tonight Show*:

> There are few things more liberating in this life than having your worst fear realized. . . . It is our failure to become our perceived ideal that ultimately defines us and makes us unique. . . . Your perceived failure can become a catalyst for profound reinvention. . . . Disappointment will come. The beauty is that through disappointment you can gain clarity, and with clarity comes conviction and true originality.[1]

Disappointment to clarity to conviction to originality. I like Conan's progression. Having your worst fears realized can be the best thing to happen to you. Because you quickly discover that the worst outcome you could possibly realize wasn't actually as bad as you thought.

So as you take steps toward your dream, ask yourself, "What's the worst that can happen?"

Usually our worst fears are not nearly as terrifying as we make them.

Once they happen, we realize they were the exact catalyst we needed all along. Our worst fears were the secret sauce to making us become better and do better work.

So if you're sitting in front of an email you're scared to send, a project you're nervous to start, a relationship you're thinking of pursuing—what's the worst that can happen? It not working out? Well, it's for sure not going to happen if you don't try.

The worst thing that can happen is you not giving it a shot at all. That would be the worst. Not a failed outcome. The worst is floating aimlessly in the ambiguous abyss of never trying and never knowing. That's the scariest place to exist.

Maybe your dream is not going to its grave right now. Maybe it's being planted. The bigger the dream, the larger the impact, the deeper your roots need to go.

If your dream is not working out according to plan, maybe that's the exact plan after all.

The Liar will tell you that nobody cares. The Liar will tell you it's not worth it anymore. Tell the Liar that ain't the truth!

Creating requires the courage to let go of certainties. If we only pursue what is certain, we certainly won't pursue much worth pursuing.

When the box you've placed yourself in shatters, after the initial trauma wears off, you realize there was a whole other world out

> **Defeat appears to me preferable to total inaction.**
> —John Adams

there waiting for you to step into it. You just needed something to smash it open. And usher you in.

NEXT STEPS:

- Look back at your own story. Can you remember times in your life when nothing went according to your plan, and yet now you can see how you ended up in a much better place because of it?
- What emotions, doubts, and questions were you feeling when your plans didn't go as expected? Write these down as well. That way, when plans go up in flames again (and they will), you will know what emotions you can expect to feel as you plan out your new plans. Even though failure rarely feels "good" in the moment, in the future it can guide you toward something more amazing than you ever could've imagined.

LIE #24

Following my dream will look sexy

After college I never moved back in with my parents. Well, that is until I was twenty-nine years old. And married. With two kids. And it wasn't my parents we moved back in with, it was my in-laws.

Let me back up. I had been working on my dream while working at my job for eight years. After almost giving up numerous times, I finally saw the door to my dream crack open just a smidge with the release of my first book, *101 Secrets for Your Twenties*, and growing momentum at my website allgroanup.com. With those eight years of trying and failing bubbling within me, by the time we actually had a real published book in our hands, my wife and I went all out with the gigantic advance I got paid for it—$5,000!

We rented a gallery in Los Angeles and threw a book launch party. The next day I flew to New York and actually paid money to speak at an event (not exactly a lucrative scenario) the night before my book officially released. I then walked back through the dark streets of New York City to the hostel room I was sharing with four other people. I remember staying up until 2:00 a.m. with nothing but the glow of my computer screen as I hammered out promotion emails while trying not to wake my hostel compatriots.

Then I flew to Chicago to speak at a joint event I set up with the group Twentysomething Bloggers, and three people showed up! Then it was off to Portland during Chris Guillebeau's World

Domination Summit and back to a Portland hostel about a mile and a half away from the event. Watching our budget drain faster than a high-powered toilet, I didn't pay to attend the conference (sorry, Chris!). Instead, I just lurked around the outdoor events and threw a Voodoo Donuts book launch party in the middle of a Portland park. Which began slow, then started going extremely well as more and more people stopped to grab a donut and check out my books! Success! That is until it started going *too* well and a Portland police officer came over to ask for my permit to sell at a Portland park. Failure! I didn't have one.

Then the last stop was a hometown wine and hors d'oeuvre event a mile away from where I grew up in Denver. All in all, we spent a couple thousand dollars to sell a couple hundred books. And I was exhausted. And the next day I was flying home to go back to work, at my full-time job, after just using all my vacation time.

So long story a tad shorter, a few months later I quit my job in marketing to go after my dream full-time. My job and my dream were not sustainable side by side any longer. One had to give. While we weren't making nearly enough money to replace my salary with my dream, my wife and I both felt like it was time to make the leap, even though we had no safety net below us and we were making the jump with a baby and one-year-old in tow.

Thus, moving in with the in-laws! Ode to joy! My wife's parents graciously opened their three-bedroom, 1,200-square-foot house to us that was already inhabited by themselves and my wife's grandmother, who was steadily losing the fight with Alzheimer's. Kids in one room. Grandma in another room. In-laws in the third room. The math did not quite add up for my wife and me to actually sleep anywhere inside.

So we helped finance (more money we did not really have) transforming the garage into a living area. I remember when we were trying to carpet the place, we literally picked up free (used!)

carpet remnants that were posted on Craigslist, and then hired a guy from Craigslist to install them for a reasonable price that then shot up by about 30 percent after he saw that we were expecting him to piece together all sizes and shapes of carpet like he was the Carpet Tetris Master of San Diego. He was none too pleased!

With my father-in-law's help, I then packed up our lives into a U-Haul on a pleasant 100-degree Los Angeles summer day where the sweet fragrance of exhaust pipes feels like it's being pumped directly into your nose. On the drive from Los Angeles to San Diego, my wife had found a free sleeper sofa that we would pass by en route (what a blessing!), which my father in-law and I picked up. We discovered that the couch had been mainly residing in this person's back porch (maybe why it was free?) and it weighed about 150 pounds (in hindsight, maybe we should have left it there!). But my wife was excited about it, so we were carrying it over fences and down sizzling hot black pavement that felt like the melting tar was going to claim my shoes with each step, to then attempt to fit the sleeper sofa into the already packed U-Haul that felt like a rolling furnace and we were trying out for a new reality show, *Jenga in Hell*!

My father-in-law wanted to meticulously unpack and repack everything in the sweltering heat, while I had every intention of just shoving that big, filthy Son-of-a-Sleeper into that truck!

Moving back in with parents. Sleeping in a garage. With pieced-together, used carpet. On an uncomfortable, and fairly-filthy-no-matter-how-much-we-cleaned-it sleeper sofa that I nearly had a breakdown trying to get home, only to have it last us one night. Two very young kids. A grandmother with Alzheimer's. One kitchen! One bathroom! But now I'm a full-time author! Let the Sexy Town of chasing our dreams commence!

If this does not appear to you and your outside opinion to be a situation set up for success, well, you'd be exactly right. But we were going for it! And if you've ever moved back in with parents as an adult, let alone also married with two kids—and for me these parents are my in-laws—plus an elderly resident with Alzheimer's, you know it's not the smoothest of transitions.

For us, let's just say the Titanic fared a pretty smooth voyage comparatively.

We stayed for eight months, which was probably about seven and a half months too long. And both my wife and I would be going to counseling soon thereafter! I ended up having the battery stolen from my car, and cables cut, twice! And I'd say that's an apt metaphor for how we felt when we left that season! Sorry I'm adding a lot of exclamation points!! Don't get me wrong, my in-laws were very gracious to let us move in as we transitioned from full-time salary to "full-time author." There were just too many intense comets colliding at once.

And when we moved out, I was so motivated that I moved all our stuff by myself for I don't know how many hours straight, jogging back and forth between the truck and stuff, and did not stop for one break until I had the back door slammed shut with every item in tow.

Phase Two of Full-Time Dream Chasing

Now it was on to Phase Two of chasing our dreams, and with book sales not exactly changing our financial lives, my wife took a part-time job back in the financial industry. With her part-time salary and the money I was making, it was still barely enough to afford life in San Diego. So my wife and I traded off working and watching our two kids throughout the day.

We went from living with her parents in their garage to living with one of her sisters in a two-bedroom condo. Again, the numbers didn't exactly add up for my wife and me as her sister slept in one room and our kids slept in the other. But thankfully the closet to the master bedroom was quite large! I think you see where I'm going here. I am not joking when I say that my wife and I slept in a closet. Attached to the room our kids slept in. And we considered sleeping in the closet quite the upgrade!

Here's a truth we learned about living in Southern California—97 percent of the population is not really affording it, but 97 percent is sure acting like they are. So we joined the masses and were not exactly promoting the fact that we were sleeping in a closet. But what do you do with all your clothes when your closet is your bedroom? Cue Ikea entertainment closets purchased off Craigslist! We filled a whole wall of the living room with floor-to-ceiling preowned Ikea-ness that housed our clothes, but a guest would think it was just a grand, trendy entertainment center.

We didn't do this as an elaborate ruse to fool guests; we did this as a way to live in a small space. But when we would invite couples over to our condo for dinner on nights her sister would be gone, we weren't exactly promoting our living arrangement. So one night when we had a couple from church over for the first time, it was with slight horror and amusement that, as my wife and I were busily preparing food in the kitchen, I heard my four-year-old daughter giving our guests the tour. I ran out right as they were entering the grand stop with my beautiful daughter tour guide announcing, "So here's the closet where my parents sleep." Oh the look of alarm, confusion, and bemusement that shimmered across our guests' faces. I think my wife had a slightly different look cascade across hers.

We lived like this for two years. In a closet. My wife working part-time. Me working on a new book, sitting in the nearest coffee shop that was about as big as the closet we slept in. And we chipped away. We raised kids. We made do. We worked. We weren't saving any money, but we were investing a ton into our future hopes and dreams.

Most of the time we must invest in sacrifice first, before we can invest in anything sexier.

167

My mom visited once from Colorado, and when we gave her the tour, a look of horror swept across her face when she realized we were sleeping in a closet. With tears in her eyes, she said, "You shouldn't be living like this." While we heard her heart for us in her sadness, we didn't see it the way she did. We saw a way of life that was allowing us to pursue something bigger and beyond our current reality.

And when we look back now at that season of living in a closet, do you know what we see? We see this sweet season of life that gave us so much freedom and was lived with such purpose.

We saw sacrifices that didn't feel too sacrificial.

That's what happens when you're creating a life that means so much to you. For us, we were making life decisions based off two big goals: (1) for each of us to be around and raise our kids, and (2) to pursue our entrepreneurial efforts and not be tied down. We were nimble.

The closet we slept in, honest to Pete, was freedom to us. Sure, there were built-in shelves over our heads with suitcases that sometimes fell on top of us. And it was great!

Sacrifice is not sexy, but it can be freeing. You're giving something up that maybe has been tying you down.

The sacrifice you're making might look crazy to others, but it feels saner to you than anything else you've ever done. Because it's purposeful sacrifice. It's going through the pain of childbirth for the gift of life that awaits you at the end.

You're not following a clear path. You're not living for the expectations of anyone else. You're intentionally sacrificing in the moment so that you can be free to do what you feel made to do in the present and future.

We were sacrificing some comforts, and in return we were getting time. We didn't have much space to live in, but we had tons of space to create and dream. That was a great trade-off, in our opinion.

No one will understand the path of sacrifice you take. All that people will see is the pain. They won't see the purpose. What seems painful to them is full of purpose and promise for you.

I watched a documentary on Toni Morrison, the acclaimed Nobel Peace Prize–winning author of books such as *Beloved*. Ms. Morrison was working as an editor at Random House, working tirelessly with authors to make their books shine. She was then also tirelessly writing her own books. She was commuting into New York to work, and she was raising two kids as a single mother. To say she was busy is probably a slight understatement.

I loved hearing Ms. Morrison describe a crossroads in her life where she wrote a list of all the things she needed to get done. She filled the page line by line with to-do's. Then as she reviewed her list, she asked herself just one question—what do I *have* to do? Slowly she started crossing things off her long list until she was left with just two things: (1) Mother my kids. (2) Write. The rest of the stuff she crossed out.[1]

She then quit her (most likely) high-salary, high-status, high-security job as an editor and she focused on those two things. Ms. Morrison had experienced quite a bit of success as an author before she made this leap, but still, it was a leap. It was a strategic leap for someone who knew very deeply who she was and what was most important to her and to the world.

It goes back to a question that I first asked in my book *101 Questions You Need to Ask in Your Twenties*: "What can you not, not do?" And when you start coming to your answer, which could take years or it could take a second (like a light switch being flicked on), it is sacrificing those things that are keeping you from your "have-to's."

And it's not have-to's by the world's standards. It's have-to's by the deep yearning and excitement of your heart and soul. Only you can answer your have-to. Yes, you can, and should, receive wisdom from others as you strive to find your have-to.

169

But you have to find, live, and sacrifice for your have-to's.

When reading about Marie-Madeleine Fourcade, one of the most effective French spies during WWII, I was struck by a line from one of her female operatives Jeannie Rousseau. She was asked by a journalist, after the war, why she had risked her life to be a spy in one of the greatest Allied intelligence coups of the war. She responded: "I don't understand the question. For me, it was a moral obligation to do what you are capable of doing. It was a must. How could you not do it?"[2]

It was a must. I love that line.

Rousseau wasn't doing what she felt she should do. She was doing what she knew she "had to" do. The sacrifice she was making was her must.

What are your "musts"? You have to find them and protect them with your life. Treat your "musts" and your "have-to's" like you would your puppy or child. You wouldn't allow your boss to come in and take your cute little Labradoodle from your house, letting you get it back when you worked there for three years and had sufficiently proven yourself.

You have to find, protect, and pursue your have-to's, or at some point you'll be wrestling with an unfulfilled life, living as you were "supposed to" instead of living as you needed to. For the health and life of your soul. For the world that desperately needs you to carry your torch and light some fires.

I don't want to live as I "should have." I want to live like I need to.

Pursuing a dream is carrying one bucket of water after another to fill a well. People won't see the 1,547 buckets you put in. They'll only see the one that made it all spill over.

The Story of Your Dream

I'm not saying you have to live with your in-laws or sleep in a closet to pursue something bigger. You could be making great

170

money and working a full-time office job and be pursuing your purpose.

But one way or another, you will be sacrificing something. Always. Sacrifice can be sexy when you're building toward something bigger. You just might be the only one who sees the sex appeal.

Sacrifice brings clarity. Because when you're giving up stuff blocking your view, you can see clearer. Sometimes you can't see the view until you remove all the junk that's blocking your window.

When I look back at our time sleeping in a closet, would I rather have been sleeping in a large, furnished room and still working my way up as a mid-level manager in a job that I can't wait to retire from forty years from now?

Or would I take that closet and now be working on my fourth book and traveling the nation, speaking to, and inspiring, others?

I'd take that closet any day of the year.

NEXT STEPS:

- What are your have-to's? It's imperative you begin answering this question. You have to find your have-to's. Maybe like Toni Morrison did, write down a list of all the things you need to do, then sit, reflect, or pray about what those things are that you have to do. Who knows, your have-to's might surprise you.

- Sacrifice can be a tad sexy when you're building toward something bigger. When sacrifice is strategic, it doesn't feel as sacrificial. So you must ask, What sacrifices do you need to make now so that you're not sacrificing what is truly important later?

- Your path to your purpose won't make sense or look very sexy to many others watching from the outside. That's okay. I call it Mount Everest Syndrome. If you started telling people you are going to climb Everest, they would think you're crazy and be trying to persuade you otherwise. But then the moment you come back after summiting Everest, they are hosting a party for you and inviting all their friends.

LIE #25

Silence needs to be filled with noise

Oh my, this is a noisy world.

—Mr. (Fred) Rogers,
in an interview with Charlie Rose

Shortly after college, I drove up to a cabin in the mountains to stay with a group of my friends. We were partaking in a *crazy* guys weekend, masterminded by our friend Sam Melvin. The whole idea of the wild weekend? To read the entire New Testament from the Bible in a day, out loud, and taking turns, and no one could talk except for the guy reading. I know, we were really some wild and crazy guys! We called it a Bible 10K.

It was a tough, surreal, freeing experience to not speak, not check our phones, and just hear all the words from the Bible read out loud. From 8:00 a.m. until 10:00 p.m., that's what we did, all of us jumping into a hot tub as the final words from Revelation came out of all our mouths in unison.

Anyway, another friend, Jeremiah, needed to leave the event earlier than most and asked if he could drive my car down the mountains. I agreed and would catch a ride later with someone else. When I spoke to my friend Jeremiah later, he said I'd almost killed him. Obviously concerned, I asked him what happened.

He told me he was listening to the radio (*Oh shoot!* I thought right away. *I forgot to warn him about that!*) when all of a sudden, as he was making a turn down this narrow mountain pass, the volume of the car radio turned itself up from 10 to 30 in mere seconds, scaring him to death as he almost lost control while he frantically tried to find the volume knob to turn it down.

My good old 1993 Honda Civic hatchback that I was given in high school and, yes, still drive today, has been turning the radio volume up by itself for as long as I can remember. It goes from smooth mellow jazz to heavy metal screaming before you know what's hit you. And when it really wants to surprise you, it turns the volume up in between the break of one song to the next so you have zero warning when that next song comes at a *make-your-ears-bleed* kind of level.

The juxtaposition of my friend Jeremiah going from this silent retreat to nearly driving off a mountain pass because of blaring, uncontrollable noise is a snapshot of our lives, isn't it? One moment we're at peace, we're calm, we feel at home in our bodies, then in an instant a headline, a social media ping, a notification, a song, an argument, breaks into the silence and smashes our peaceful home with noise.

One moment we're driving through the mountains, admiring the beauty all around; the next we're distracted and almost swerving to our deaths.

Silence is a revolutionary act. You are revolting against the clanging and banging of the world that is screaming at you to listen. When my car radio is blaring, I can't choose not to listen. I'm only choosing survival as I desperately try to turn down the volume while not crashing into the person in front of me.

As the Grinch lamented, "Oh the Noise! Noise! Noise! Noise!"[1] Maybe he was Grinch the Wise and was hearing something we hadn't caught onto yet?

Someone Stole My Car Radio

You ever heard the song from Twenty One Pilots about the lead singer Tyler Joseph's real-life experience of someone stealing his car radio and now, he sings in the song, he just sits in silence? He sings about the battle he now faces of complete silence and having to think for himself in the quiet, instead of hiding behind all the noise. Watch the video of the song to experience what I think is a powerful, intense metaphor of how this battle is playing out for many of us today. Because like singer Tyler Joseph confesses in the song, "I liked it better when my car had sound."[2]

We are purposefully drowning ourselves. In noise. Every day. Why? Maybe the lie is, at the heart, that we won't like what we hear. Maybe we're constantly filling the loneliness and fear inside us with noise so we won't feel alone and afraid, which in turn, makes us feel more lonely and fearful than when we began.

Why would we rather be struggling for air and barely surviving than taking deep breaths and being filled with life? When my car radio is turning itself on high, I can't think of where I'm going. All I can think about is survival.

All the Noise

So much talking and so few good conversations. So much shouting and so little listening. So many headlines and so little understanding of the fine print. So much noise and so little silence.

Maybe we're not having any breakthrough ideas in our lives because we haven't allowed any time or space for an idea to break through.

Maybe we feel far from God because we never have a conversation with him where we actually listen.

Maybe we feel the world is a hateful and terrible place because we keep listening to the voices screaming at us that the sky is falling.

175

> Our society is much more interested in information than wonder, in noise rather than silence. . . . How do we encourage reflection? . . . Real revelation comes through silence.
>
> —Fred Rogers to Charlie Rose

Why are we surprised that we have a scarcity of clarity?

How can we expect to have any peace in our lives when we constantly keep inviting all the angst of the world to fill our home and constantly shout at us everything that is going wrong? Noise doesn't even have to be audible. Noise can be nuanced. A silent assassin of sorts—a glance at our phones as we see the latest terrible headline or a quick scroll through all social media posts and how our lives are not measuring up to theirs. This creates noise inside our heads and hearts, cascading through us in a wake of anxiety and fear that drowns our peace and confidence.

When I write, I find myself, as I'm doing right now, being drawn to a spot next to a lake. Looking over the ripples with the only noises being the moving water and the call of birds, funny enough, I can actually think. The screaming grows silent and I can actually hear.

More and more in today's world, the most radical choice you can make is to choose silence. To be still and know.

Because no technology, no politician, no company, no product, no advertisement wants you to make this choice. Silence is free. Silence is freedom. A freedom to be, and think, and find rest and peace. And no one can sell you something there, when you're willing to choose something free and freeing. I believe the only one who can "sell" you something in silence is God. And he's going to "sell" you peace, worth, value, clarity, revelation, truth, wisdom, and love. All free things worth more than anything.

In silence you trade your anxiety for peace. In silence you trade your confusion for clarity. In silence you trade your loneliness for a rooted sense that you're never alone. In silence you can take the problem and find an answer. In silence the Liar's voice is revealed for what it is as the Truth-Teller's voice has a place to speak. In silence the answers come from within instead of being force-fed to us from the outside world.

As I watch Fred Rogers speak with Charlie Rose, I'm in amazement as I watch Charlie Rose voice his awe for this man in front of him.

"You seem to me to be the calmest person I know," Charlie Rose says. "You have a quality that is reassuring. . . . I'm surely not as centered as you are and I can look at you with envy and astonishment because there's something to be admired about the life you've lived. Mine is much more frenetic. I'm much more about gulping in as much as I can find. I want to see everything, do everything, feel everything."[3]

And as we look at the life of Mr. Rogers and the fruit produced, and the life of Charlie Rose and his fruit, I am convicted as well at the stillness, sureness, and deep wisdom that pours from Mr. Rogers' presence, even in front of the camera. Juxtaposed with Charlie Rose, who jokingly admits that he's a "hopeless case"— the frenetic man who is on a desperate search for "more," next to the man who is still, silent, and at peace in his lack of noise.

Mr. Rogers speaks very slowly and intentionally. And when you watch *Mister Rogers' Neighborhood*, you almost feel like he's constantly forgetting his lines. Because there's so much silence, and on a TV show, silence is death, which why they call it "dead air."

But when you watch Mr. Rogers, he's perfectly at peace in it. And as I learned through different interviews about Mr. Rogers,

> What is essential is invisible to the eye. The closer we get to understanding that truth, the closer we get to wisdom.
>
> —Fred Rogers

he's purposefully speaking slowly because he is strategically giving the kids watching the space and silence to think about what he's just said. He's giving the kids the space to think for themselves. He's not cramming the answer into them. He's giving them the freedom to wrestle with the question. In "dead air" there is so much life!

Maybe, in the end, that gift of silence and reflection as an invited guest into Mr. Rogers' home is the greatest gift he gave us all.

In your twenties, with so many major life decisions to make, are you giving yourself this same gift? Are you giving yourself the space for stillness and silence? Are you giving yourself the time to think and reflect about what is important to you in this life? Clarity and conviction are birthed, not adopted. Your soul has a lot to tell you if you will listen to it.

The details of your day have a lot to speak to you if you will pay attention to them.

Charlie Rose then goes on to talk about how many high-flying friends he has and how they want to achieve big things, have a high status, make a lot of money, and then, yes, still do something bigger than themselves. Mr. Rogers quietly smiles at Charlie Rose's story, then responds, "All I know is that when I walk out of the studio someday and there is a child that has Down syndrome, for instance, and that child comes up and gives me a hug, I know that's the field I want to be growing in."[4]

Mr. Rogers dug a deep well. Mr. Rogers filled himself with truth and wisdom, and then fed his TV show audience with it every single day.

So I guess the question we must all ask ourselves is this: how badly do we really want clarity in our lives?

Are we lying to ourselves, telling others we're desperate to find the answers to our relationships, career, calling, and purpose, when in reality we won't take five minutes to really seek any of the answers? We must expose this lie, and if we're not willing to do

> If you have a garden and a library, you have everything you need.
> —Cicero

something about it, we can at least stop blaming the world or God for the lack of peace and clarity in our lives.

We used to live annoyed by distractions. Now, too often, I think we live for them.

There's too much riding on this decade of your life to have it be blown out in constant noise. What is worth more to you? To constantly be "in the know"? To constantly be up-to-date? Or is it worth more to you to know deep down what your worth is?

When we allow ourselves to constantly be overwhelmed by noise, then it is impossible for us to hear. And maybe, in the end, is that what we want? Do we want to drown out the possibility to think and really reflect because we're afraid of what we might hear?

Silence speaks to your well-being, not your well-doing.

The well within you. Your being. Are you filling it with junk or are you filling it with water?

I want to have a deep well like Fred Rogers. I want to speak, listen, and love from that well. And I'm not sure I will be able to dig a well very deep if I'm using the internet, social media, and the TV as my main tools.

This chapter is not me calling all of us to live as monks, or to scrap the world as we know it and go back to carrying a pager on our hip. All I'm suggesting and contemplating in my own life is, how do we cultivate stillness even in the middle of chaos? To seek out "silent silos" throughout our day. Whether for just a few minutes or much longer. As we cultivate the gift of silence, then we can be still and at peace while in the noise of our day.

My home is rarely quiet. Having four kids under eight years old is like having four different radios on at the same time, volume turned on high, all playing different genres of music, with each "radio host" demanding that you pay more attention to them than the other three radios! So as I cultivate reflection and fill my well-being, I'm better able to really hear what all these cute little precious radios are really saying. I'm better able to hear the music than the noise.

To be still. To know. To pray. To listen. At night, when our kids are asleep and still, I sneak into their rooms to cover them with a blanket. And I pray over them in the silence of sleep that they will know who God is in them and who they are in God. I pray over them a deep knowing.

To find silence in the noise. To find peace in the frenetic.

This will only become harder and more important for our generation and the generations to come. The noisy world will only get noisier. Most days I drive around with my car radio off. It is my only defense against the volume turning up on its own. Sure, I could get it fixed, but I guess I've liked the silence.

So can you revolt right now?

Can you sit in silence? For five minutes and just be?

What do you hear?

NEXT STEPS:

- Can you be more intentional to find "silent silos" throughout your day? Taking a five-minute walk break outside at work. Spending some time in the quiet of the early morning. Going on a hike, getting into nature and listening to what your soul is telling you. These silent silos will speak more to you than anything else you'll hear all day.

- Clarity is birthed, not adopted. We find clarity not somewhere out there but from within.

- The noisy world will only get noisier. How can you be more intentional at blocking all the noise? The world doesn't want you to be silent because it can't sell you any-thing there.

- If your well-being is sick, your well-doing will be flimsy, flammable, and forgettable. Dig a deep well with reflec-tion, reading, meditation, and prayer. No matter what new technologies come along, these tools will always be better at digging a deep well within. You can't dig a well with an iPhone.

FINAL CHAPTER
The Twentysomething Declarations

Twenty-five lies! There they are. Now as we look further toward moving away from these lies and into truth, here's what I believe should be 25 twentysomething declarations we can replace these lies with.

25 Twentysomething Declarations

My name is _____.

My life hasn't gone exactly as planned.

Yet, as I strive to live and breathe wisdom, joy, and truth in my twenties, here are 25 declarations I will live by.

1. I choose to live intentionally. For far too long I've lived intentionally unintentional. I must keep moving forward to figure out where in the world I'm headed.

2. I choose to believe that I owe the world, instead of believing that the world owes me.

3. No more nostalgia. No more wishing I could go back to some time when I didn't have any "problems." Nostalgia is a liar. There were always problems. Each season carries with it the good, the bad, and the ugly. I choose to be present in my present and envision my future as I work toward

it, more than I obsess about the past. If I see the good in every season only after the season is over, then I will never actually see any good.

4. I choose hope over cynicism.

5. I choose community over isolation. I'm not alone in this.

6. I choose to create instead of complain.

7. I will be open to opportunities that initially look like roadblocks. Dead ends are only dead ends if I turn around.

8. When I find myself opening the fridge after 9:00 p.m., I'll ask myself these questions:
   - Am I thirsty?
   - Am I tired?
   - Am I bored?
   - Am I anxious?
   - Maybe I'm not hungry after all?

9. I won't try to escape frustration. I will dive headfirst right into it. I will let the frustration of **"This is not where I want to be"** cattle-prod me where I need to go.

10. When I begin to feel the lure of Obsessive Comparison Disorder kicking in, anxiety swelling inside me like a balloon being filled with Mountain Dew, I will say out aloud, "Not me. Not tonight!" I will turn off the TV. Put down my phone. And read a book. Or pray. Or call a good friend. Or go on a walk. I will thwart Obsessive Comparison Disorder and Obsessive Connection Disorder before they thwart me.

11. The goal of my life will not be to live comfortably. Comfortable is a quicksand. I will keep moving forward or agree to sign the waiver that I understand the risk of being suffocated by perks, 401ks, and office birthday parties.

12. I choose to get lost on purpose with purpose for a purpose. I can't explore if I don't first lose site of the familiar.

13. I will not blame others. No one is to blame. The more I blame others, the less I move forward. Blaming others for my situation is like swimming in circles in a murky pond. No matter how hard I swim, I'll end up in the same place, covered in muck.

14. I will not expect others to solve my problems. I will ask myself the tough questions.

15. I will not expect a relationship to solve my problems. I will ask my relationship the tough questions.

16. I will not go to social media to complain. Complaining on social media is like spraying yourself in skunk, then wondering why everyone tries to avoid you.

17. I will not fill every down moment with the smartphone. How can I think for myself if I'm obsessed with reading the thoughts of everyone else? I will not avoid awkward situations by escaping into my phone.

18. I will love from my strengths and not from my insecurities.

19. I will allow myself to be at peace if I choose to be home on a Friday night. And Saturday night too. I will not feel less because I choose not to continually chase more.

20. I will sing loudly. Dance unashamedly. And live unapologetically big while being faithful in the small.

21. I'll floss more often. For real this time.

22. I will read books. Good books. That give me life. I repeat. I will read books. Good books . . .

23. I choose not to allow social media to validate or invalidate me.

24. I will listen more than I talk. I will seek to understand instead of trying to force others to understand me. I will

show people they are important by asking good questions, putting my phone away, and just being present with them.

25. I will serve the world by serving it the best of who I am. I will not let these lies and the Liar take me down anymore. My future will take time. I will keep the hope.

FINAL, FINAL CHAPTER
Last Words of Encouragement

Thank you for walking with me as we've explored the lies that hold us back in our twenties. Our twenties are hard. Removing these lies and clinging to truth will make this decade more purposeful and give us a strong foundation to build on.

As we part ways and walk out into the unknowns ahead, here is my prayer for you.

I pray that you will know that you're enough even when it feels like you're not accomplishing much of anything.

I pray that staring at the blank white walls in front of you won't overwhelm you, but will give you the excitement to pick up a brush and paint.

I pray when all the lies try to slime you that you will run through cleansing water like a kid running through sprinklers on a summer day.

I pray you will let the Truth-Teller guide your life instead of the Liar.

I pray that you will listen to that small, still voice inside you that is screaming to be heard.

I pray that you will be filled with peace even when the world feels overrun by the contrary. I pray you will let yourself be still and know. I pray you will seek silence even in the middle of the storms.

I pray you will define, refine, own, and hone who you are.

I pray that you will create. That you will walk through your day expecting to see something amazing. You're living in a masterpiece. All you have to do is take notes.

I pray that you will give yourself grace in not knowing what you're doing while you sometimes ungracefully figure out what to do.

I pray you'll have the courage to change. That you will never know the cold, confused complacency of thinking you've got it all figured out. I pray you'll forever be the student and not stay frozen under the lie of "making it."

I pray that you'll leave your phone out of the bathroom when you sit on the toilet because you don't have to be online every second. And come on, I might need to borrow your phone someday and that's just gross.

I pray that the heavy weight of all the unknowns will feel surprisingly light.

I pray that the next movie you stream will actually be worth your time.

I pray that when a friend calls, you will pick up the phone even when it doesn't feel like the right time to talk. Because for many years in your twenties it might not feel like the right time to talk.

I pray you'll see that maybe God is not ignoring you when it feels like God is not answering your prayers for all the big things you're crying out for. Maybe God is saving your life.

I pray you will see God working even when you can't see anything growing out of the dry ground.

I pray that you will mentor and be mentored. That you will intentionally seek out those whom you can help and those who might want to help you.

I pray you won't give up.

I pray that you'll look a few people in the eyes this week and tell them how much you love them.

I pray that you will war for hope, treating hope as a fact, not a fleeting feeling.

I pray that you *won't* need to hit rock bottom before you begin your descent back toward truth. I pray you will cling to wisdom as the lifesaver it is.

I pray that you will truly embarrass yourself once this year going for something that you feel completely incapable of attempting. And that you'll realize that the embarrassment wasn't that embarrassing after all.

The next time you do a belly flop, I pray you'll see that God is waiting there, ready to wrap your hurting body in a big warm towel.

I pray that when you feel like you've got nothing left, you will realize that you've got so much more.

I pray that you'll know when it's time to run and when it's time to crawl. When it's time to work in a cubicle and when it's time to light it on fire. (Figuratively speaking, of course.)

I pray you'll know what season you're in. When it's time to plant and when it's time to harvest. I pray you'll keep working the ground.

I pray you'll pursue big things without worrying too much about immediately having big results.

I pray joy will envelop you like a fresh pile of laundry out of the dryer.

I pray victory over every loss.

I pray life. I pray truth. I pray hope. I pray all the ashes will be made into diamonds.

This is my prayer for you.

Big Thank-You's

First, thank you to everyone who read this book and made it here. If you have questions for me or just want to reach me personally I am here at paul@allgroanup.com. I seriously value and appreciate every conversation I get to have with readers.

Thank you as always to my amazing wife, Naomi, who, like every book before, edited every page of this book before any other eyes could take a glance. What a wild ride it was on this one too! I think back to you editing the book at a playground while I attempted to watch all four kids, as our one-year-old tried to climb things with a cast on her arm, when we had left our house for people to come in and view it because we were trying to sell it, all while a national emergency was announced for a global pandemic! You know looking back, that was slightly intense! But we made it, with a big thanks to you!

Thank you to all my children—Hannalise, Sierrah, Judah, and Jlynn—for being a constant source of inspiration and encouragement to find joy and truth in life. I love each one of you dearly.

Thank you to my dad, Louis Angone, for providing a place of encouragement to bounce ideas off during our biweekly bocce ball games. Thank you as well for letting me win so many games to keep my morale up. (Sorry, had to ☺)

Thank you to the Downing House for being a special place of rest, reflection, and service. Thank you to John Irwin and the amazing staff of the Downing House for putting me up, and putting up with me, for a few really productive days. If not for my time there, I'd still be about halfway done with the book. Thank you as well to the Blank Family for being amazing family friends and letting me stay at your place to write.

Thank you to my agent Chad Allen for all your hard work and amazing direction you gave me while we bounced around from one book proposal to another. You were a true source of wisdom and encouragement throughout the whole process. I'm very thankful that our paths recrossed at the time they did. I think this whole agent thing looks good on you.

Thank you to my editor Brian Thomasson at Baker Books for making this book better. Thank you for your diligence to clean up the mistakes and push me to go deeper, all while possibly editing this book from the back of your pick-up truck in your garage as you searched for a silent space to work amidst all the kids being home. I'm pretty sure you deserve an "I Edited a Book during a Global Pandemic" medal or ribbon. I'll look into that.

Thank you as well to copyeditor Barb Barnes for your incredible diligence in all the details and breathing so much clarity into each chapter. Plus, I really think you did a really great job actually taking out all my actuallys! And all my repeating word repetitions. ☺

Thank you to the rest of the team at Baker Books for your diligence in moving this book forward during a tough time in our world. I'm excited to be working with all of you and getting to know you more.

And as I've done with each book, thank you to all the musicians who encouraged me to keep writing and creating while I worked on this book. I drew a lot of inspiration from Jon Bellion to think deeper and keep pushing myself. Thank you, Jon! You are a gifted musician and writer who brings a level of authenticity and originality to your music that prodded me to try and do the same. I opened up a lot of writing sessions by going way back to "Transatlanticism" by Death Cab from Cutie—a magical and weirdly inspiring song for me. The poignancy of "Car Radio" by Twenty One Pilots was a source of inspiration in the book itself. Loved stumbling across the band Jungle, which was an energy boost while writing. "Rut" by the Killers is a powerful song and video that I found myself writing to in many ways.

Finally, thank you again to you, the reader, who has now actually read all the way through the acknowledgments section as well! You should be given a medal or ribbon, or both. I'll look into that too. Seriously, thank you. A book is not much of a book without an amazing reader like yourself. You look great today, by the way. Did you do something different with your hair?

Notes

Lie 3 I'm the only one struggling

1. Michael Bond, "How Extreme Isolation Warps the Mind," BBC Future, May 13, 2014, https://www.bbc.com/future/article/20140514-how-extreme-iso lation-warps-minds.
2. Keron Fletcher, quoted in Bond, "How Extreme Isolation Warps the Mind."

Lie 4 I've missed my chance

1. Allan Cunningham, *The Poetical Works of Robert Burns* (New York: Alden, 1883).
2. Fred Schruers, *Billy Joel* (New York: Three Rivers Press, 2015).
3. Schruers, *Billy Joel.*
4. Tim Robbins and Morgan Freeman in *Shawshank Redemption*, directed by Frank Darabont (Culver City, CA: Columbia Pictures, 1994).
5. Quotes from Morgan Freeman as "Red," in *Shawshank Redemption.*

Lie 5 None of this matters

1. Interview with Elie Wiesel, *U.S. News & World Report*, quoted in "Insight: Perspectives on the World," *Arizona Republic*, October 26, 1986, C6.
2. Robert D. Putnam, *Bowling Alone: The Collapse and Revival of American Community* (New York: Simon & Schuster, 2000), 341.
3. Paul Angone, *101 Secrets for Your Twenties* (Chicago: Moody, 2013), 36.

Lie 7 I better get mine

1. Erich Fromm, *The Sane Society* (New York: Open Road Media, 2013), 360.
2. C. S. Lewis, "The Weight of Glory," *The Weight of Glory and Other Addresses,* ed. W. Hooper (New York: Simon & Schuster, 1996), 25–26.

3. Chan Kim and Renée Mauborgne, *Blue Ocean Strategy* (Boston: Harvard Business Review, 2004).

Lie 8 I deserve to be happy

1. Yasmin Anwar, "Happiness Hyped, Ethnic Competition, and Power Poses," *Berkeley News*, February 10, 2014, https://news.berkeley.edu/2014/02/10/spsp conference2014/.

Lie 9 Everyone is doing better than me

1. Sherry Amatenstein, "Not So Social Media: How Social Media Increases Loneliness," PSYCOM, 2019, https://www.psycom.net/how-social-media-increases-loneliness/.
2. Jason Colditz et al., "Social Media Use and Perceived Social Isolation Among Young Adults in the US," *American Journal of Preventive Medicine*, 2017.
3. Gregory Spencer, *Reframing the Soul* (Abilene: Leafwood Publishers, 2018).
4. Samuel Gibbs, "Apple's Tim Cook: I Don't Want My Nephew on a Social Network," *Guardian*, 2018, https://www.theguardian.com/technology/2018/jan/19/tim-cook-i-dont-want-my-nephew-on-a-social-network.

Lie 10 I'm not good enough

1. Backstage Staff, "Dustin Hoffman Recalls His 'Graduate' Audition," *Backstage*, 2006, https://www.backstage.com/magazine/article/dustin-hoffman-recalls-graduate-audition-34679/.

Lie 11 I need to stay constantly connected

1. Turkle, *Reclaiming Conversations*.
2. Alice Walton, "Investors Pressure Apple over Psychological Risks of Screen Time for Kids," *Forbes*, 2018, https://www.forbes.com/sites/alicegwalton/2018/01/09/investors-pressure-apple-over-psychological-risks-of-screen-time-for-kids/#844fd7b38dfe.
3. Elizabeth Dilts, "Apple Says It Looks Out for Kids, as Investors Cite Phone 'Addiction,'" *Reuters*, 2018, https://www.reuters.com/article/us-apple-shareholders-children/apple-says-it-looks-out-for-kids-as-investors-cite-phone-addiction-idUSKBN1EW0WS.
4. Tony Fadell, Twitter, 2018, https://twitter.com/tfadell/status/950329842196721664?lang=en.
5. Neil Postman. *Technopoly: The Surrender of Culture to Technology* (New York: Knopf, 1992), 6.
6. Turkle, *Reclaiming Conversations*.
7. Interview with Fred Rogers, with Charlie Rose, "Remembering Mr. Rogers." YouTube, posted 2016, https://www.youtube.com/watch?v=djoyd46TVVc.
8. Nancy Kanwisher, as quoted in Nicholas Carr, *The Shallows* (New York: W. W. Norton and Company, 2010), 29.

9. "Sour Mood Getting You Down? Get Back to Nature," Harvard Health Publishing, July 2018, https://www.health.harvard.edu/mind-and-mood/sour-mood-getting-you-down-get-back-to-nature; and Rob Jordan, "Stanford Researchers Find Mental Health Prescription: Nature," Stanford News, June 30, 2015, https://news.stanford.edu/2015/06/30/hiking-mental-health-063015/.

Lie 13 I'm such a failure

1. Scott Johnson, "Oscar to Suicide in One Year: Tracing the 'Searching for Sugar Man' Director's Tragic Final Days," *Hollywood Reporter*, 2014, https://www.hollywoodreporter.com/news/searching-sugarman-director-dead-thr-710882.

2. Maya Angelou, quoted in Amanda Macias, "15 Pieces Of Advice From Maya Angelou," BusinessInsider.com, May 28, 2014, https://www.businessinsider.com/maya-angelou-quotes-2014-5#:~:text=%E2%80%9CSuccess%20is%20liking%20yourself%2C%20liking,of%20the%20other%20virtues%20consistently.%22.

Lie 15 Nostalgia

1. Chloe Grace Moetz, *500 Days of Summer*, directed by Marc Webb (Century City, CA: Fox Searchlight Pictures, 2009).

2. Interview with Joseph Gordon Levitt, with Larry King, "It's Tom's Fault," YouTube, posted April 3, 2019, https://www.youtube.com/watch?v=MWUCMrFcMcM.

Lie 16 But I worked so hard

1. Paul Angone, *101 Questions You Need to Ask in Your Twenties* (Chicago: Moody, 2018), 82.

Lie 18 God, or the universe, is against me

1. Psalm 23:1–4.

Lie 19 Nothing good can come out of this

1. Corrie ten Boom with Elizabeth and John Sherrill, *The Hiding Place*, 35th anniv. ed. (Grand Rapids: Chosen Books, 2006).

2. Ten Boom, *Hiding Place*, 210.

3. Elie Wiesel, Acceptance Speech, NobelPrize.org., Nobel Media AB 2020, Sept. 28, 2020, https://www.nobelprize.org/prizes/peace/1986/wiesel/26054-elie-wiesel-acceptance-speech-1986/.

Lie 21 I'm well-informed

1. Rebecca Clements and Trevor Haynes, "Dopamine, Smartphones, and You: A Battle For Your Time," Harvard, 2018, http://sitn.hms.harvard.edu/flash/2018/dopamine-smartphones-battle-time/.

2. "Chamath Palihapitiya, Founder and CEO Social Capital, on Money as an Instrument of Change," YouTube, Stanford Graduate School of Business, 2017, https://www.youtube.com/watch?v=PMotykw0SIk.

3. Thomas Merton, *Confessions of a Guilty Bystander* (New York: Penguin, 1966), 238.

4. Hans Rosling and Anna Ronnlund, *Factfulness* (New York: Flatiron, 2018), 9.

5. Giovanni Luca Ciampaglia and Filippo Menczer, "Biases Make People Vulnerable to Misinformation Spread by Social Media," *Scientific American*, 2018, https://www.scientificamerican.com/article/biases-make-people-vulnerable-to-misinformation-spread-by-social-media/.

6. Adam, Arvidsson et al., "Good Friends, Bad News—Affect and Virality in Twitter," *Future Information Technology*, 2011, 34–43.

7. Rosling, *Factfulness*.

8. Eric Schmidt, quoted in Eli Pariser, "Beware of Online Filter Bubbles," TED Talk, 2011, https://www.ted.com/talks/eli_pariser_beware_online_filter_bubbles.

9. Shahram Heshmat, "What Is Confirmation Bias?" *Psychology Today*, 2015, https://www.psychologytoday.com/us/blog/science-choice/201504/what-is-confirmation-bias.

Lie 22 It needs to be perfect

1. Peter Guralnick, *Sam Phillips: The Man Who Invented Rock 'n' Roll* (New York: Little, Brown, and Company. 2015).

2. Guralnick, *Sam Phillips*, 165.

3. Guralnick, *Sam Phillips*, 165 (emphasis added).

4. Guralnick, *Sam Phillips*, 292.

5. Pharrell Williams and Maggie Rogers, "Pharrell Williams Masterclass with Students at NYU Clive Davis Institute," YouTube, NYU Clive Davis Institute, 2016, at 18:15, https://www.youtube.com/watch?v=G0u7lXy7pDg.

6. Maggie Rogers, "Alaska," "Pharrell Williams Masterclass," at 20:35.

7. Guralnick, *Sam Phillips*, 206.

Lie 23 What if it doesn't work out?

1. "Conan O'Brien's 2011 Dartmouth College Commencement Address," YouTube, Team Coco, 2011, https://www.youtube.com/watch?v=KmDYXaaT9sA.

Lie 24 Following my dream will look sexy

1. *Toni Morrison: The Pieces I Am*, Magnolia Pictures, 2019.

2. Jeannie Rousseau, quoted in Lynne Olson, *Madame Fourcade's Secret War* (New York: Random House, 2019), xxiv.

Lie 25 Silence needs to be filled with noise

1. Dr. Seuss, *How the Grinch Stole Christmas* (New York: Random House, 1955), 9.

2. Tyler Joseph, "Car Radio," Twenty One Pilots, Regional at Best Records, 2011. See https://www.youtube.com/watch?v=92XVwY54h5k&ab_channel=Fueled ByRamen.

3. Charlie Rose, "Remembering Mr. Rogers (1994/1997)," YouTube, 2016, https://www.youtube.com/watch?v=djoyd46TVVc.

4. Rose, "Remembering Mr. Rogers."

Paul Angone is one of the most trusted and sought-after voices in the nation to college students, young professionals, and those going through career change. The bestselling author of *101 Secrets for Your Twenties* and *101 Questions You Need to Ask in Your Twenties*, Paul is a dynamic keynote speaker at universities, corporations, and churches nationwide. He is also the creator of AllGroanUp.com. He lives just outside of Denver, Colorado.

JOIN PAUL ANGONE OVER AT
ALLGROANUP.COM

Your twenties and thirties are hard and important.
All Groan Up is a community dedicated to reminding
each one of us that we're not alone.

This *Groan*-Up life isn't simple or straightforward, and
we need a safe, real, hilarious space to talk about it.
Can't wait to see you there!